hopeNwork.palestine@gmail.com ◉◉◉◉ @ hopeNwork.palestine
☎ +962 77 9 134 134

The Blessed Land 1
(The Story of Palestine and its Cities Haifa and Safed)
By: Osama Alshayeb & Somaya Almomani

First Edition
Published in 2018 by the authors
Copyright ©The Authors

All RIGHTS RESERVED. No part of this book may be reproduced or transmitted in any form by any means, electronic or mechanical, including photocopying and recording, or by any information storage and retrieval system, except as may be expressly permitted in writing by the authors.

Idea, preparation and supervision:
Osama Fahmi Alshayeb | Somaya Mahmoud Almomani

Written by: Somaya Khouja

Illustrated by: Jinan Nassar

Palestinian Heritage drawings by: Rasha Afifi

Arabic Proofreading by: khadra Tayyem | Dr. Sultan Al-ajlouni

Translated by: Ala'a Mismar

Designed and directed by: Osama Alshayeb

References:
Many visual and reading references were used in documenting the information, images, and events that appeared in the story.

Dedication

I dedicate this humble work to:

My parents

who had supported me through their prayers.

My faithful Wife Somaya,

my soul mate, who had stood by my side all the way ever since we started this project.

My daughters, son, brothers and sisters

who had lift up my spirits and encouraged me to finalize and deliver this book.

Izz-Aldeen Abu Dahrooj,

my best friend, for his care, follow up and support.

To ALL others who stood by my side with their advice, ideas and wisdom

I thank you all from the bottom of my heart

Yours: **Osama Alshayeb**

Table of Contents

Dedication	III
The story of beloved Palestine	01
Haifa, the big hope	12
The First scene	16
The Second scene	18
The Third scene	22
The Fourth scene	26
The fifth scene	28
The sixth scene	32
The seventh scene	36
The eighth scene	42
The ninth scene	44
The tenth scene	46
The eleventh scene	48
The twelfth scene	52
The thirteenth scene	56
The fourteenth scene	60
The fifteenth scene	64
The sixteenth scene	68
The seventeenth scene	70
The eighteenth scene	74
The nineteenth scene	76
Lessons learned from the story of Haifa	80
Questions about the story of Haifa	82
Safed, the galilee lily	86
Introduction	88
The first scene	90
The second scene	92
The third scene	94
The fourth scene	98
The fifth scene	100
The sixth scene	104

The seventh scene	106
The eighth scene	110
The ninth scene	114
The tenth scene	118
The eleventh scene	122
The twelfth scene	126
The thirteenth scene	130
The fourteenth scene	134
The fifteenth scene	138
Lessons learned from the story of Safed	142
Questions about the story of Safed	144
Terms and definitions of the story of Haifa and Safed	147

VI

THE STORY OF BELOVED PALESTINE

The story of beloved Palestine

When the evening came and the cool stunning breeze was moving around, when the night silence prevailed showing its shining stars so wide, a big smile showed up on the innocent faces of the three siblings a smile they don't want to hide. It's time for the nice and brilliant stories; as the kind grandma has finished her prayers and sat beside the raging fireplace which sends some fire sparkles to the boiling sage kettle that is waiting for Rajaa's hands to give it a pinch then sip it with the amazing flavored cake that their grandma prepared earlier.

Everything is silent, even their breath and souls, Jihad, Salah and Rajaa had come. The girl put some sage sticks inside the boiling kettle and the nice smell spread all over the place, the grandma smiled as a sign of satisfaction. She felt comfortable to start telling her exciting story in an intelligent metaphoric manner. She started, as she always used to do, to tell them the story of Arab and Muslim countries, countries of Glory. Telling them some beginnings, salute champions and give hope. She told them stories that moved around the earth and dwelled in the sky. From Haifa the bride she started, then Safed the historical pure and steadfast land. Akka, the high white walls. Besan, the land of water, palm and grapes trees. Nazareth, civilization, elegance and growth. Jerusalem, oh you blessed land, al Aqsa mosque gives you highness and superiority. Oh Palestine, accept our love and appreciation, from you we shall start and at your territories we shall return, to be attached to your pure soil. In your Biography wonders, comfort and cures are found.

Grandma said: before we start our story I'm going to tell you a brief introduction about Palestine, so you can know everything about it my dear grandchildren. Palestine, my dears, is the heart of the Arab world, and loyalty should be to it. God has blessed this land since ever, it is the land of celestial messages lots of messengers had lived and died in this land. On this land the most important historical events had occurred side by side with the history of the greats.

The first dwellers were the (**Arab Jebusites**) They migrated from the Arabian Peninsula and settled in the area of Jerusalem, which was called «**Jebus**», then the **Canaanites Arabs** migrated and settled in the plains of Palestine and in the hills, and other tribes of them have inhabited the mountains.

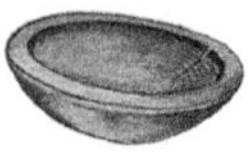

Palestine was initially called the **Land of Canaan**, referring to the Canaanite Arabs of origin. This was clearly stated in the celestial books, the Torah and the Bible. History here has the final speech: At that time, the Jews had no existence and were never mentioned.

Salah asked his grandma: and how was Palestine given its actual name granny?

Grandma answered: This is due to people who migrated from an area called «***Plast***» they were titled with courage and strength.

They chose the **Canaanite** Palestinians as their neighbors, and they got mixed with their language and cultures, and melted by the will of the Beneficent. Since then, beloved Palestine has become their name. A name printed in the heart and conscience, can anyone blame!

Palestine was ruled by lots of civilizations and people, some of them corrupted it and some of them built it with all glory and respect, until the duration of the honorable Muslims came, they built it with all love and harmony, and spread justice among all its inhabitants, their rule extended for 1100 years, and for long centuries, everyone lived under their rule peacefully, even the followers of other religions such as Jews and Christians.

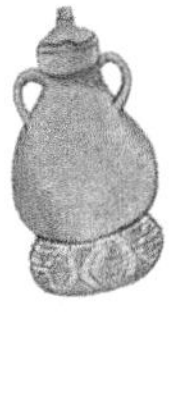

Jihad asked: How dare the Zionists to occupy the land of Palestine, our ancestors land?

Grandma replied: a few number of Jews lived in Palestine peacefully side by side with Palestinians after they had recourse to them and found warmth and joy, they found good and generous people, fertile land and excellent geographical location and serenity. The greed of **the Zionists** to occupy Palestine began and spread like a disease after the Second World War and the British colonialism had come.

The British colonization published a declaration called **Belfour,** to surrender Palestine to **the Zionists.** After they withdrew from it and left the borders. "The promise of those who do not have the right to those who do not deserve such promises." They worked to facilitate immigration and vow to the Jews. And to grant them Palestinian lands illegally and ungratefully.

The Zionist immigration began to increase, to the steadfast land of Palestine, and began to settle and steel the fertile lands, houses and wealth with all its arrogance, without paying any attention neither to its indigenous inhabitants nor to their heritage, their rights or their origin.

Since then, the tragedy of Palestine and its painful plight began, when the unjust military force has overshadowed the natural and legitimate right of the oppressed people to accept injustice or immorality.

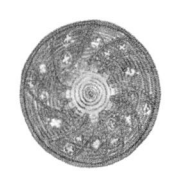

The siblings wondered, is it possible that Palestinians accept to leave their own land? Of course not, replied the grandma. Haven't I told you before that Palestinians do what they say?

The Palestinian refused to sell his land or give it up, and so are the honorable ones. The war broke out in Palestine in 1948. It was a bloody year, when the blood of innocent people was shed, and the Palestinian people did not spare any effort, they know how to defend!

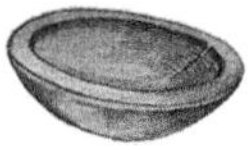

The Zionists forcibly displaced many of Palestinian people under the threat of arms, cruelty and injustice. They demolished the houses above the heads of its inhabitants, and neither the shouting nor the call was heard, and the rebellious youth were arrested and many of them were executed but with their Lord they are still alive!

They seized the empty houses without mercy, and then a Zionist entity rose on a land covered with the blood of the martyrs. The sky cried. Palestine, you are still the beloved and you are the symbol of dignity and pride!

They have enacted unjust laws and tried to Judaize the territories in various ways, but ancient history, civilizations and various groups testify to the rightful owners of the land. Long terms do not give thieves the legitimacy to own what was stolen.

Has the story of Palestine ended?

Never, as long as our hearts beat with love and desire to hug its soil, and the Palestinians continue in all ways and do not diminish from seeking to return to their land and their obvious right, and the rights of their ancestors and children. Injustice must be cleared.

It will never end, whoever remained there struggled to keep his land, and whoever was abroad inherits the story of beloved Palestine for his generations, and tells them the story of his struggle. The journey of return will not stop until the right returns to its owners.

It will never end, indeed, there is an initiation, from Haifa we start, Haifa the pampered Palestinian bride and the sword in the face of the oppressive occupation, if I were to talk about it, then books and newspapers will be filled, but our hope will be fulfilled with hard work to make an introduction for future stories.

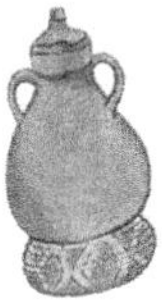

Here the grandma stopped talking, and yawned quietly in an announcement of the end of this cold evening story, especially that it turned dark and the three brothers felt sleepy. It was few seconds before they were asleep leaving the story of Haifa for tomorrow with its events and heroes as an interesting fantasy and dream.

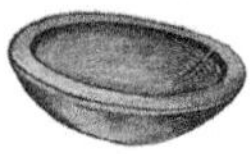

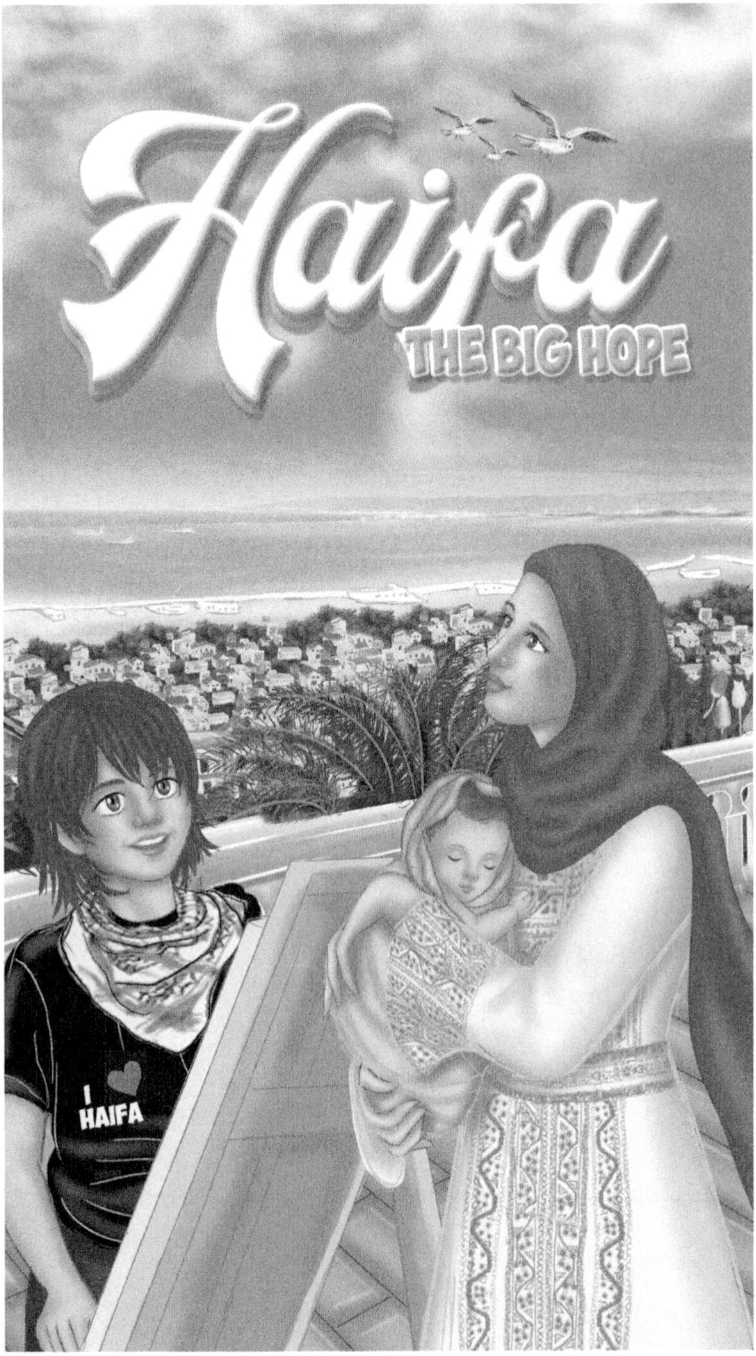
Haifa
THE BIG HOPE
I HAIFA

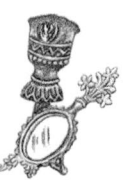

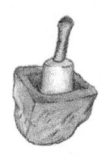

HAIFA
THE BIG HOPE

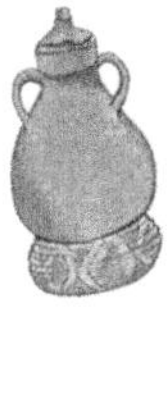

The beautiful evening came again, and the brothers gathered around the grandmother waiting for more to gain, from the beautiful tales with a unique selection, where they can find wisdom and magnificence and useful information!

The grandma started her story wondering,

Who is our hero Hasan? From where he came? And how he demonstrated the necessity of hard work to fulfill our hopes and dreams?

It is Hasan, the dreamy boy, who dreams to be (Hasan Al Din Alfalastiny) in an imitation of the hero (Salah Al Din Alayyuby).

Our hero lives in his beloved city Haifa, in a valley called (Wadi al-Nesnas)..

He was helping his grandfather in cultivating olive seedlings to make the Arab neighborhoods a paradise after the Zionists took off their trees. He knew that unrelenting work, and knowing more about his homeland are the real hope for him, his family and the children of the neighborhood to establish the roots of patriotism in the confused souls. His intelligence and great hopes that he is trying to achieve based on his trust in God at the first place, then his belief in his right to return his occupied land enabled him to achieve positive steps like when he helped his older sister Asma'a in making a gallery to use its income in building an Arab school in his beloved city of Haifa.

THE FIRST SCENE

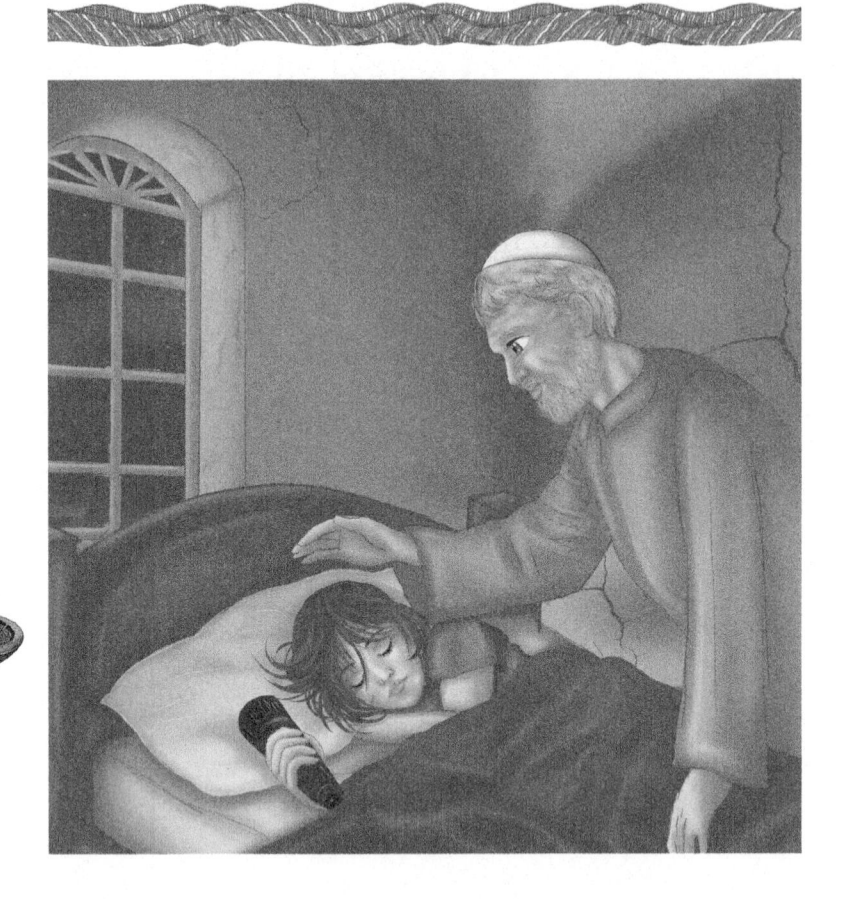

The old man approached his grandson with caution, wanting to take the flashlight from his hand.

Hasan was in a deep slumber, but he held on to his lamp vigorously, and within seconds he opened his eyes for a little and said with a low voice:

Grandpa, it doesn't bother me, keep it with me if you don't need it.

Grandpa (smiling): How do you wake up so quickly, son? They've cut off the electricity, and I want to check the External hose.

Hasan: it's okay, when you're done, leave it to me at the edge of the window, please.

He closed his eyes and slept again. He spent the last two days moving stones to repair their garden wall that was about to collapse.

THE SECOND SCENE

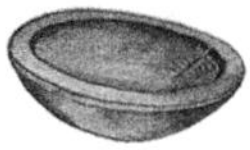

Hasan woke up smelling the fresh **Saj bread's** (Stone made bread) aroma that covered all his home's parts. That smell was mixed with a special smell; the smell of **Zaatar** (thyme). He loves **Manakish** (Zaatar pies) and can never get bored of eating them.

Hasan: Good morning my beautiful mom. Where's grandpa? He promised me to bring some new seedlings to grow them together today. We should meet at **Mount Carmel**.

Mother: Good morning my son, your grandpa went out in the early morning. He has a conference with some men from our neighborhood. They are looking for a solution for the frequent and intentional power and water cuts.

Hasan: sure… they think that such cuts can force us to get out of this valley, but alas! We are here steadfast.

Hasan headed to the oven where his mom was sitting with her cheeks getting blushed because of the oven's heat. And there he sat squatting with his hand on his face, watching the bread; once getting baked and puffed on that metallic tin, and another between his mom's hands who was professional in making the dough getting thinner and thinner while moving it from hand to another. Her beautiful smile never left her lips. That smile that filled up her original **Palestinian legacy kitchen.**

Hasan had his breakfast, kissed his mom's head and took her permission to leave in order to meet his grandpa at **Mount Carmel.**

THE THIRD SCENE

ואדי ניסנאס
وادي النسناس
Wadi Nisnas

Hasan did not forget to fold two loaves of Manakish bread before he took his flashlight from the edge of the window, Then he hurried towards (***Mount Carmel***).

Hasan, a 10-years-old boy, lived with his small family in a very old Arab house in a valley called (***Wadi al-Nisnas***), which is the most prominent remaining Arab neighborhoods after the occupation of the Zionists of Palestine, the age of this valley is more than six hundred fifty years. People live under difficult conditions because of the limitations the occupation set by cutting off water and electricity, and ban them from repairing their homes.

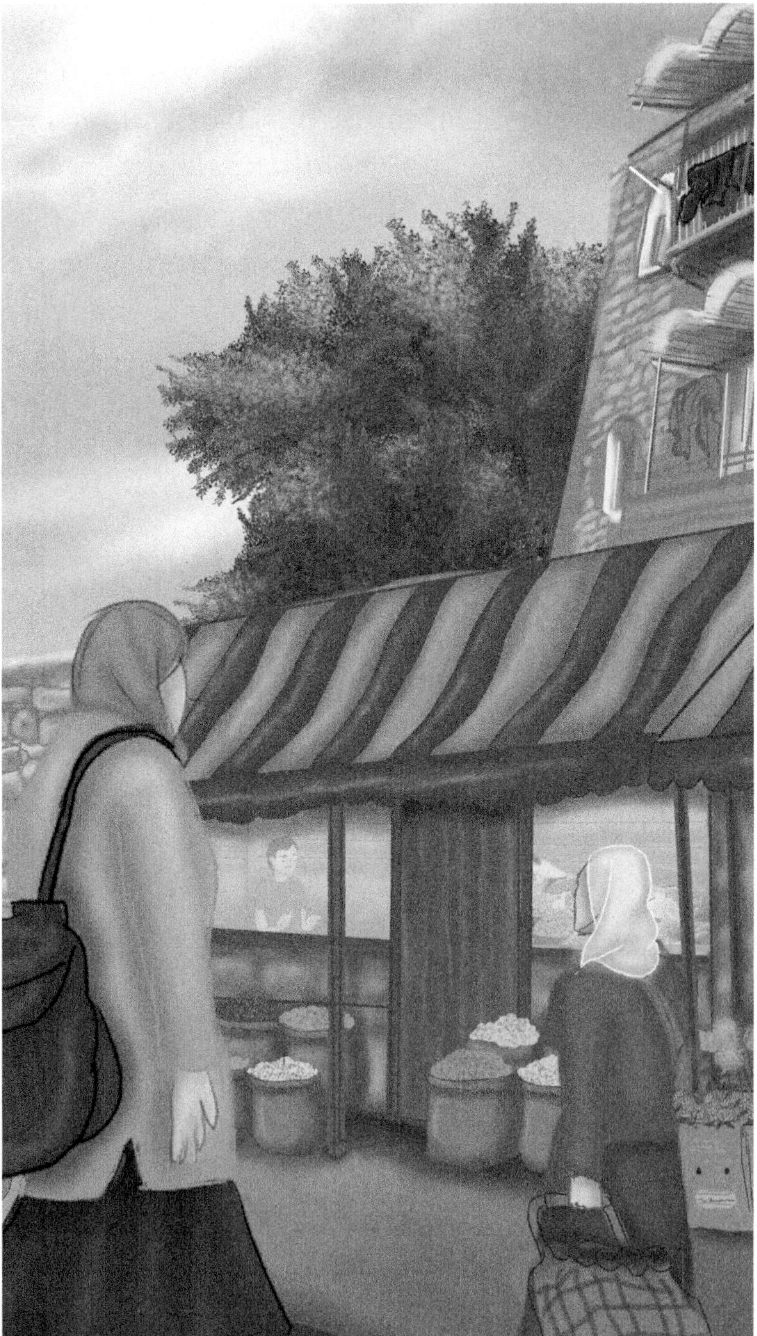

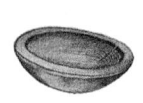

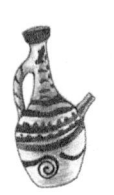

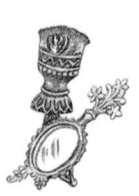

His dad was an owner of a small grain shop in which he used to sell whole grains and beans. Hasan visits this shop from time to time, but he loved the sea and loved to collect shells, and was hoping to go on a cruise with his uncle Samih, who works in fishing and owns a big boat, to collect enough shells before the arrival of his eldest sister Asmaa from Kuwait, she has been absent for five years, after she got married and traveled there, and finally she will be able to come, to establish the promised exhibition.

THE FOURTH SCENE

As soon as Hasan arrived at **Mount Carmel**, he stood in front of a big forest, and entered from a small distance between attached trees into his secret hiding place, he gazed at his painting with the light of the lamp on it, to write with his coloring pencils those small letters.

Hasan: Thanks God, I'm about to finish, I still have to add large shells on the edges and some coloring.

He heard his grandfather calling him, left his pens, and his shells, and hurried out to him.

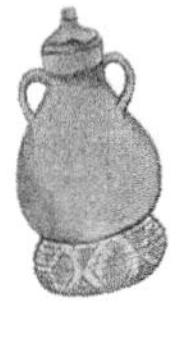

THE FIFTH SCENE

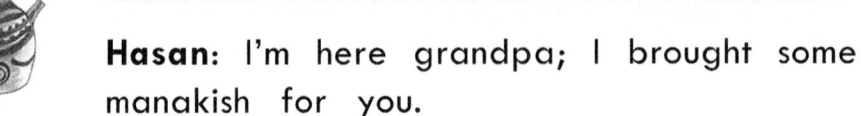

Hasan: I'm here grandpa; I brought some manakish for you.

Grandfather: I already had my breakfast, why you are that late my son? I was waiting for you to start cultivating the new olive seedlings.

Hasan: oh really? And how many seedlings are we going to grow?

Grandfather: eight; as a total we have...

Hasan interrupting his grandpa with enthusiasm: twenty four seedlings.

Grandpa: Hahaha, you are intelligent son, actually you are smarter in calculation than me.

Hasan: When the plants grow and become trees, we will move them and grow them around the house as a make up for the trees that were taken off by **the Zionists**; we will make our Arab neighborhoods a paradise again.

Grandpa: Yes, my son, our roots in this blessed land are as deep as the roots of the **fig** and **olive** trees, we are Arab **Canaanite** Palestinians in origin, no matter how **the Zionists** tried to blur our language or change the names of our streets, neighborhoods and markets. Steal our ancestor's civilization and historical monuments, and you, son, with your energy and intelligence, are our hope for a bright future, God willing.

Hasan: I learned that from you grandpa. My father used to tell me how skillful you were in memorizing multiplication table before the age of school. And how you memorized poems and loved to read and write in your youth. Many of your articles have been published in the (**Carmel newspaper**), in which you always warned of the danger of Zionist migrations to our land and owning some of the surrounding neighborhoods with the support of British colonialism.

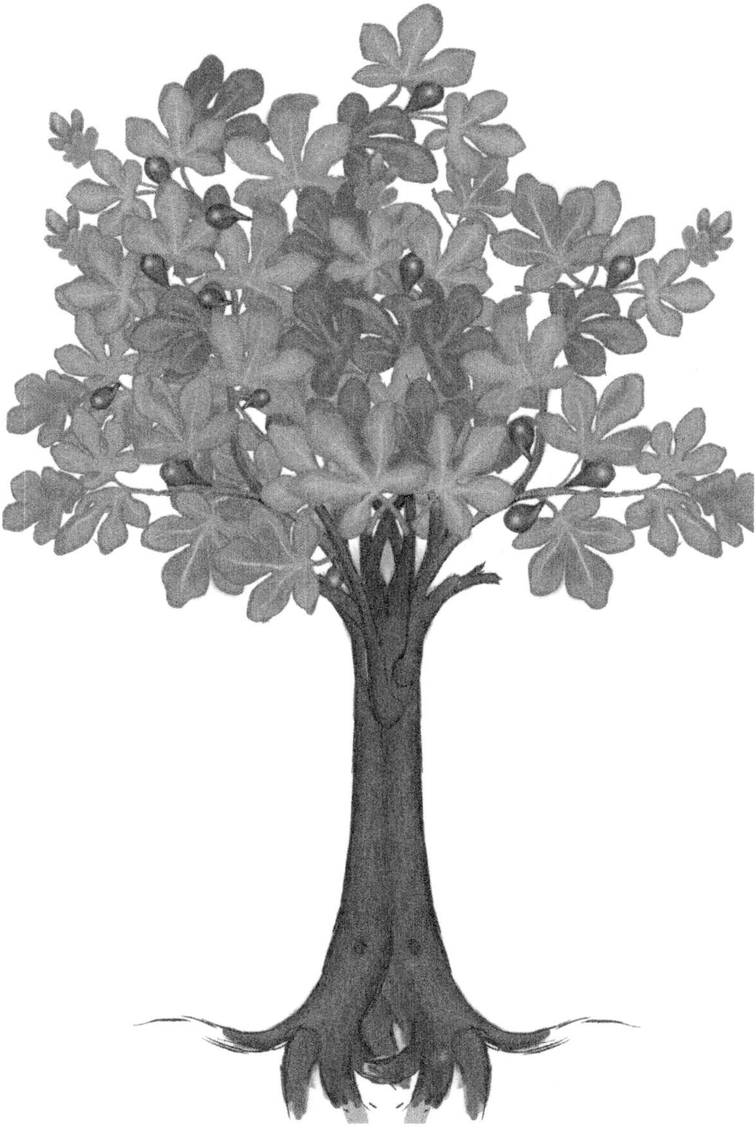

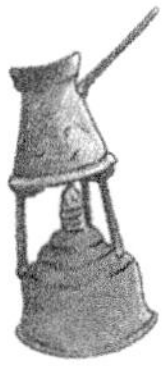

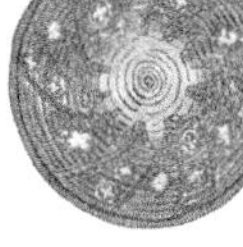

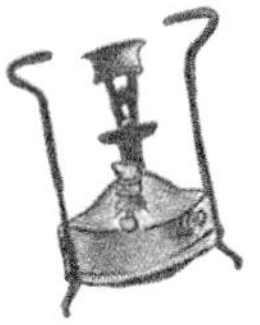

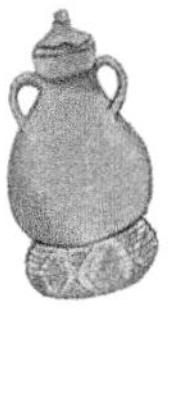

THE SIXTH SCENE

Grandpa: yes my son, that's how our ancient city was. Haifa residents were well-known about their energy and challenging spirits. They also were developed in architecture. Their sources of income varied leading to a flourished Haifa in various fields.

Hasan: how was that development grandpa?

Grandpa: they reached high levels of development; they established an industrial school to teach people some occupations such as carpentry, blacksmithing and car repair. Arab and foreign schools were deployed there.

The National Library was the first public library to be established in Haifa. It was full of different types of books, folders and various historical references. It has become a lighthouse of science for people from the Arab countries to come to participate in their cultural, social and sport activities.

Hasan: every time you talk about Haifa I feel more in love with it, and more proud of its history.

Grandpa: you will always be proud of it son, besides, Haifa was a sparkle of Islamic call, and its impact is important in urging people to resist the colonists. I can't forget (**The Istiqlal Mosque**), which is still elevated from the time of its martyr leader (**Izz al-Din al-Qassam**) to this day.

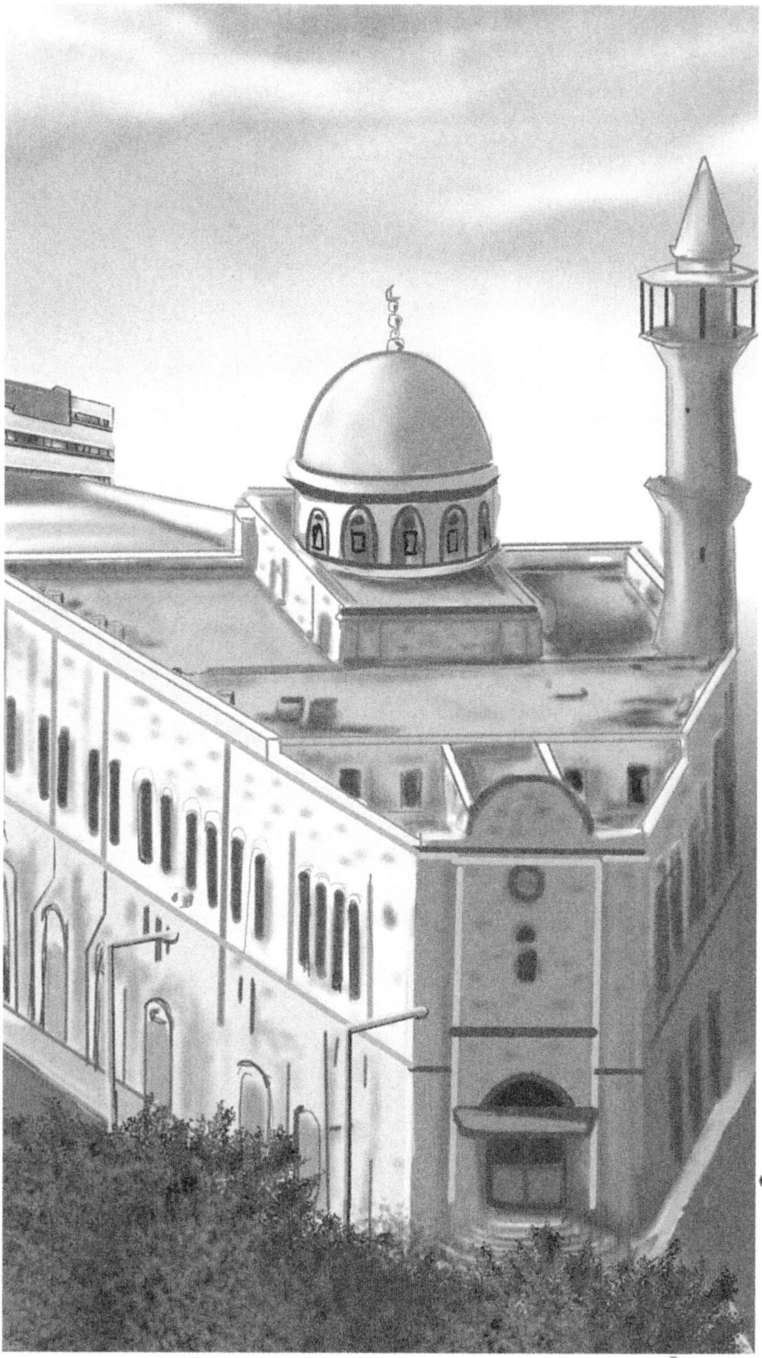

THE SEVENTH SCENE

Hasan: Grandpa, you made me curious to know more and more about Haifa, its neighborhoods and people's lives.

The grandfather smiled and said: oh darling, you reminded me of the beautiful past, when people were living side by side a simple and spiritual life, they had no leader but union, peace and harmony.

Some of them were plowing the land, others were engaged in fishing and sea journeys, and others were knitting and making shoes and bags. The rest were stick to their shops in their small market in the (**old town**) selling and having fun, happy and contented with what God Almighty offered them of the Halal livelihood.

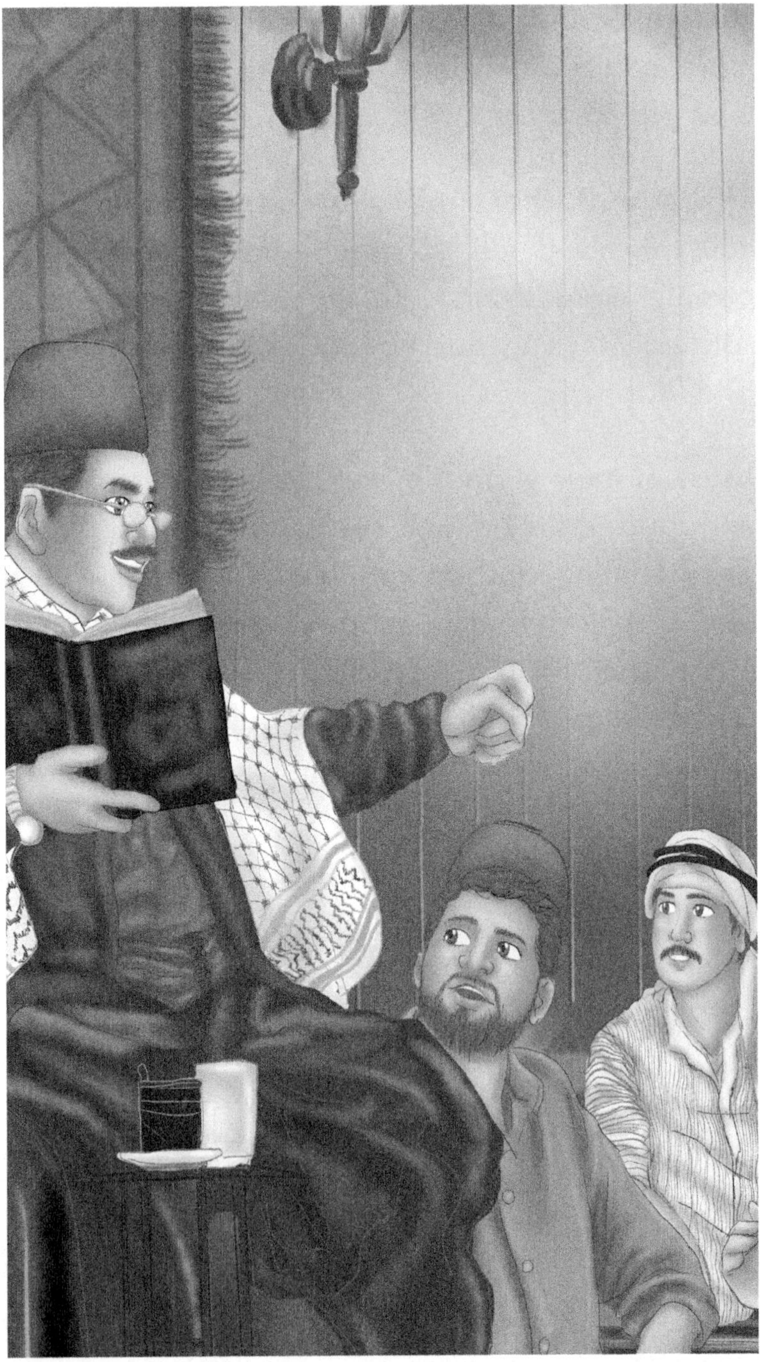

That city was hilarious with both its modern and old neighborhoods.

I feel nostalgic to the "**Al-Hanatir Square**" and the **Old Town** markets, when the **Hakawaties** (story tellers) walked around the neighborhoods presenting funny stories in their simple Palestinian language.

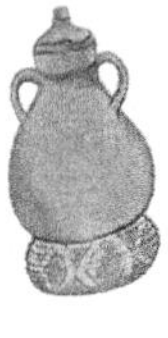

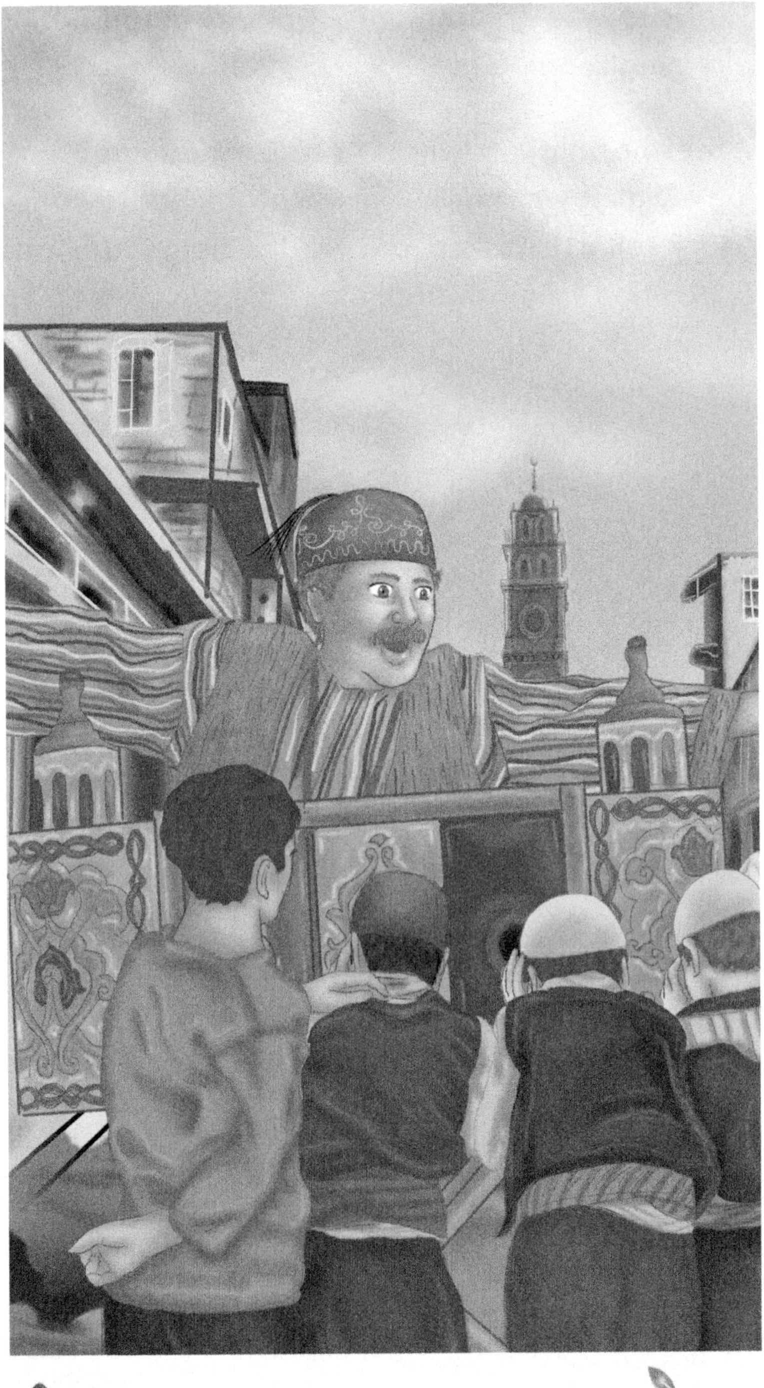

Woe to the box of wonders and its wonders! Yet the man with the beautiful embroidered tarboush (red cylindrical hat) calls out to the children with his beautiful voice:

Come and see. See the wonderful life.. Ohh..

Come and let go..

And forget your sorrow..

From Istanbul to Sindh..

And Beirut at the End...

Stories and tales..

And hidden world wonders...

He shows them pictures of the Arab and Islamic landmarks, and the beautiful cities of Palestine with its beautiful nature and sacred and ancient places.

THE EIGHTH SCENE

Hasan sent a long sigh holding his breath and wondering: how were you able to build this architecture and civilization in this short time, grandpa? And who is this genius builder? I'm really confused.

42

The grandfather smiled for Hasan's sigh and replied: "He is the sheikh (*Zahir al-Omar*). He built it on the Palestinian coast to protect it from the land and sea invaders. He built a wall and four towers, with two gates one heading to the city of Jaffa and the other to the city of Akka, Haifa enjoyed its stability and security at his time, also trade and urbanization started to develop.

Hasan: was Haifa the first modern city built by a Palestinian Ruler?

Grandpa: Yes, my son, Haifa has become the starting point for a modern and developed city opened to the three continents (Asia, Africa and Europe).

Hasan: how great you are Haifa!

THE NINTH SCENE

The grandfather grabbed his grandson Hasan hand with pride and drove towards the **Nasr Grand Mosque** (known as **Juraina Mosque**) to perform Duhr (noon) prayer there.

On the way, Grandpa smiled, and began to tell his grandchild their smart idea of liberating the mosque after its closure for many years since the occupation of the city by **the Zionists**.

Grandpa: when the occupation arrested **Sheikh Raed Salah** in 2003, the city's youth set up a large tent in the courtyard of the mosque, congregational prayers were held and the young people protested there. This drew people's attention to it (the mosque) and the number of its visitors increased. In 2011, we restored the mosque despite the attempts of the desperate occupation to close it, and so, victory was our ally.

Hasan (wondering): doesn't the minaret look strange with its urban nice shape?

Grandpa: It is strange, my son, that **the Zionists** destroyed the real minaret of the mosque, without any respect for the sanctities and religions. What you see now is the **Clock Tower**, one of seven towers established in various Palestinian cities, in the era of **Sultan Abdul Hamid II**. As you see, it is an archaeological building; it has six floors with a clock hanged on each direction before being stolen by the colonists. At that time, it was one of the highest towers in the city, today it serves as a minaret for this ancient Mosque.

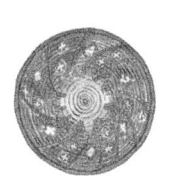

THE TENTH SCENE

Haifa, that ancient Canaanite city, was blessed with its warm beauty, large and wide, with a view of (**Mount Carmel**), which means (God's generosity). This mountain extends from Haifa to the mountains of **Nablus**.

The green colors there send hope to souls especially that it was decorated by shining **red windflowers (known as Hannoun or Dahnoun)** spread all over the mountain; making it more beautiful, fresh and joyful. The gradient green rekindles beauty and ability in souls. There are plenty of **oak trees** and you can notice the breeze touching the tree's leaves and hear their rustle. Then happily take a look to the water where the Mediterranean Sea is stretched before you flowing with light and shining blue. Its water reflected the golden sun, it looks bright shiny along the beach, as if it's a painting of a creative artist, How not? It is painted by God, the illustrious with all creativity, uniqueness and ability.

THE ELEVENTH SCENE

In the next morning, from the beautiful **Hakoora** (house yard), the father completed the repair of the large gate, putting some *jasmine* branches to extend over it, and his eldest son Mohammed helped him extending the colored lamps through it, then Abu Mohammed sat down after his work drinking tea, enjoying the birds singing and

48

twittering as if it was talking to him and telling him pleasant news. The phone rang and the man knew that it was an outside call, he picked up the phone quickly and eagerly, to hear the voice of Asmaa; what made him cheerful. She told them that she will arrive after three days; and her vacation may be prolonged a bit; until she delivers her baby.

The whole family was happy with that news, and began to prepare for the reception of Asmaa and her little daughter Sarah, who had been slightly over two years old.

While Hasan started to encourage people to finish their paintings if they want to participate in the Wadi al-Nisnas exhibition. He worked for hours to finish his painting. He wants to surprise his sister Asmaa, his family and the people of the neighborhood.

THE TWELFTH SCENE

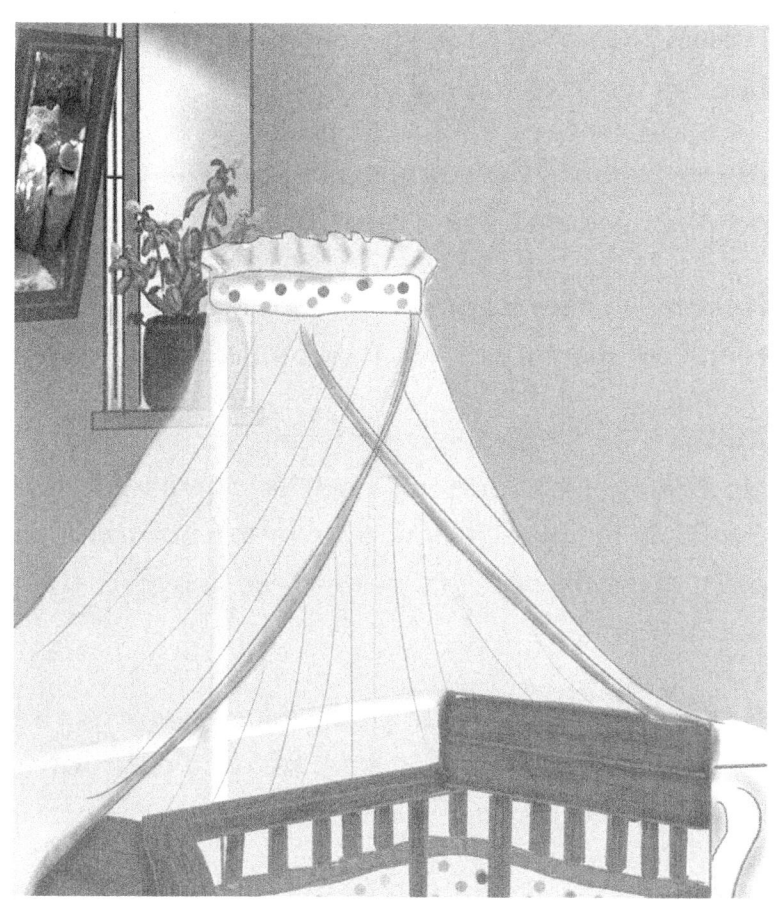

Mohammad's mother took Hasan's old bed out of the basement and wiped away the dust while smiling joyfully.

Hasan: when is the dinner time? I'm starving.

Mom: calm down, nothing bad will happen to you. Wait until I finish what I'm doing, and then I'll prepare you the dinner.

Hasan: mom, isn't this my old bed, my mattress and my beloved blanket?

Mom: hahaha! Oh yeah, and now it will go to the new baby, aren't you happy for Asmaa's visit?

Hasan: I'm very happy, I can't wait to see her and recall our memories and stories together.

Mother: Can't anyone miss his childhood, his home, his family, his freedom, and his homeland that dwells in his blood? Son, to love the homeland is part of faith, and this is what we learned from our religion.

Hasan: yes mom, I wish people know how much I love this place! I think I will not be able to breathe if I leave this place.

Mom: huh, have you become a fish son?

Hasan: I wish I were a fish, mommy, so that I can swim in the beautiful sea of Haifa, and sink in the depths - and whispered Inside- and gather enough shells to complete my craft.

Hasan helped his mom taking the bed out. They put it in Asmaa's old room, which was crowded of here paintings. The mom collected the paintings and took the biggest one and hanged it on the wall.

Hasan: What a beautiful image of this brave hero, my mother, isn't he who liberated the city of Haifa and many of the Palestinian cities from the hands of the Crusaders in the Battle of Hittin?

Mother: Yes, my son, he is the hero leader (**Salah Al-din**), after his death; the Islamic state got weakened and the Crusaders occupied it again, the conflicts remained until the king (**Khalil Ibn Qalawun**) came and liberated it. Haifa remained under the rule of Muslims until the **Nakba of Palestine.**

THE THIRTEENTH SCENE

Hasan: what do you mean by *"**Nakba of Palestine**"* mom?

Mom: in 1948, the Zionist Haganah gang surrounded Haifa from its four sides; they began firing heavy guns and machine guns at the residents. They forced people to leave their homes and leave the port by force of arms and threats, and then they started to steal houses. They stole everything son, money, furniture, old books even important manuscripts written hundreds of years ago. Then they built a fence around (***Wadi al-Nisnas***) for the remaining people and prevented them from going out for two years unless they get permission, the valley became a large prison. The Zionist occupation of our city and other Palestinian cities continues to this day.

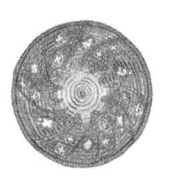

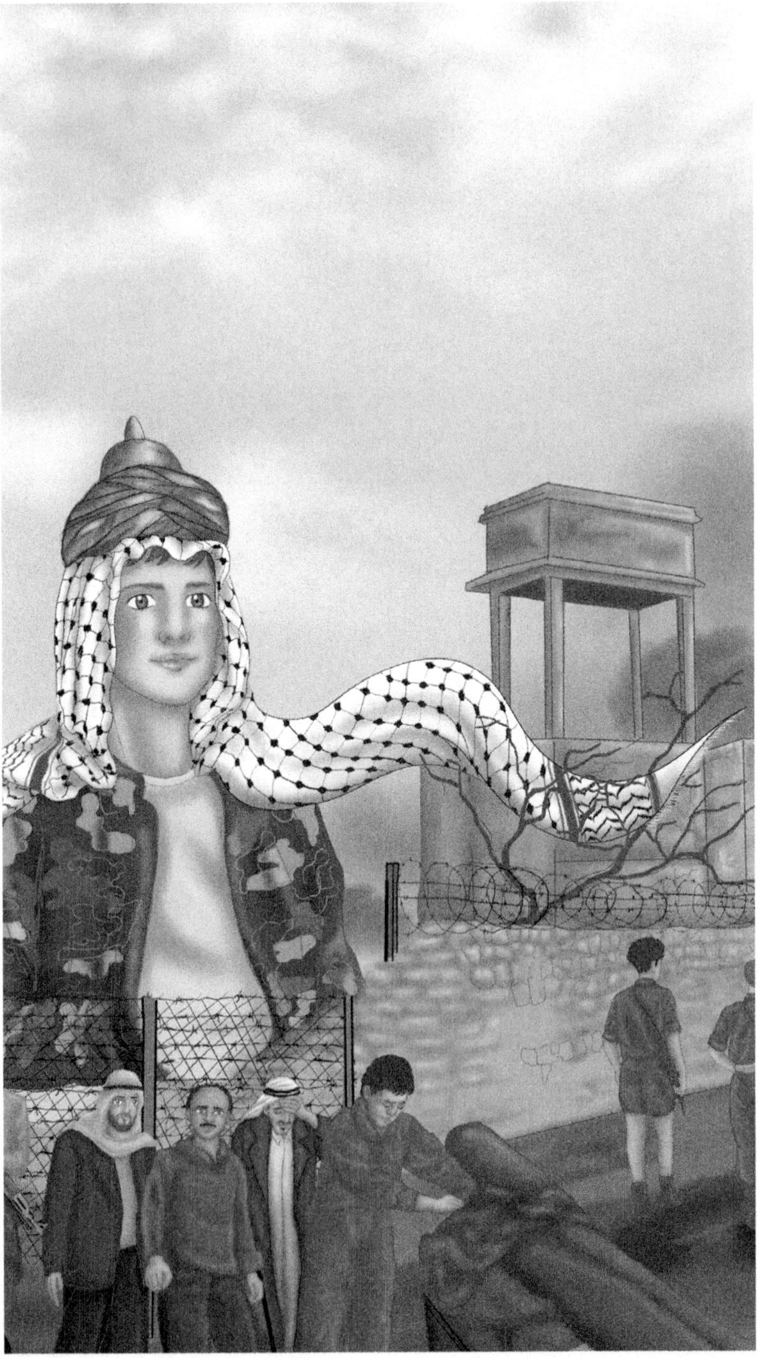

Our ancestors resisted the occupation with all their possessions, but the strength of **the Zionist's** army and their developed supplies were way greater than what the inhabitants had.

Hasan: when I grow up I'll be (**Hasan Al-din Alfalasteny**) I'll force all the Zionists to leave the Palestinian mountains and valleys. And return the raped houses and give them back to their real owners. God welling! You will see it, Mom, as you see me now.

I believe in that mom, we will build mosques, homes, schools and hospitals again. We are the right owners, and right is always the victorious.

THE FOURTEENTH SCENE

Silence dominated for a while, and then Hasan grabbed his mom's hand and continued his talk denying this despicable occupation.

Hasan: why they occupied our country mom? And what is the importance of our city? There must be a secret behind that.

His mother patted Hasan's shoulder tenderly and whispered: we believe, son, that despite the hard situation Palestinians are witnessing, they will return to their homeland which they were forced to leave, victorious. As long as this country has people like you.

She continued, Haifa before the **Nakba** was one of the most important Palestinian cities. Attracting labor and traders from Syria, Lebanon, East Jordan and North Africa, it became an important commercial center, and the gate of Palestine to the world, it was famous for the export of grain and the transfer of goods thanks to its big port and deep water. Ships and cruises came from all over the world; it was considered the second most important port between the Mediterranean ports.

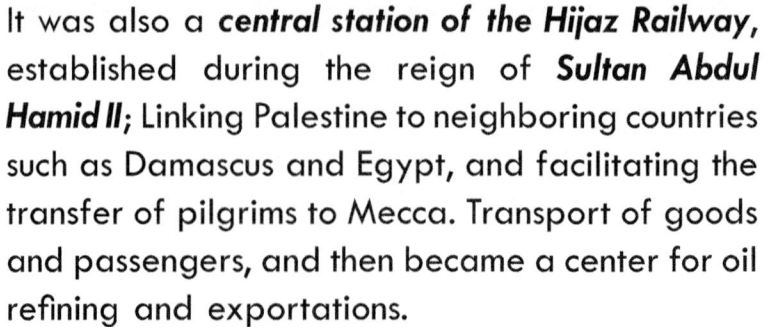

It was also a **central station of the Hijaz Railway**, established during the reign of **Sultan Abdul Hamid II**; Linking Palestine to neighboring countries such as Damascus and Egypt, and facilitating the transfer of pilgrims to Mecca. Transport of goods and passengers, and then became a center for oil refining and exportations.

Hasan: All this in my beloved Haifa!! .. It is something to be proud of mom, my appetite is increased. Come on, let's go together to have dinner.

THE FIFTEENTH SCENE

The next morning, the sun shone on the people of the beautiful city, carrying them warmth and love, and sending its tender rays to the roses, which are lined by the sides of the roads and balconies, and heading towards the water of the sea and increase the glow and beauty reflecting on its calm surface, giving hope to the hearts of young and old people.

Everyone in the house woke up on the doorbells, Abu Mohammad hurried to open the door, he found his daughter Asmaa standing in front of him Smiling with her beautiful brown face, and beside her a little girl of the most beautiful and sweetest eyes he had ever seen, he felt very happy and embraced his daughter into his arms tenderly.

Dad: welcome my dear daughter, thanks god you are here!

Asmaa: Thank you my best father in this world, I miss you very much, I missed my mother, my brothers, i missed the smell of the aromatic basil.

She looked at her mother who stood aside with her cheeks full of tears of joy, and mumbled her mother's words on her wedding day:

Put henna on my hands,
Make me bright with candles..
Prettify me with thyme branches,
I wish to hug you and walk with pride..
What a good luck I have,
Come on mom hug me tight!

Both daughter and mom had a prolonged hug, then Asmaa started to kiss her mom's head and hands, they cried and left no limits for their tears, then she kissed her grandpa and hugged her siblings.

Hasan stood still, barely holding his tears. Then he grabbed Sara's hand and took her outside to show her the iron swing that belonged to him long time ago. He painted it with beautiful colors as a sign of welcoming her.

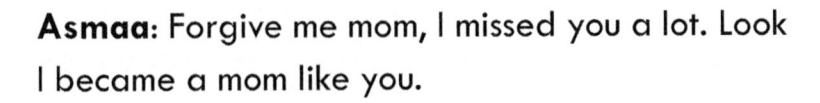

Asmaa: Forgive me mom, I missed you a lot. Look I became a mom like you.

Mom: you are the most beautiful mom my daughter, you and Sara are welcomed home.

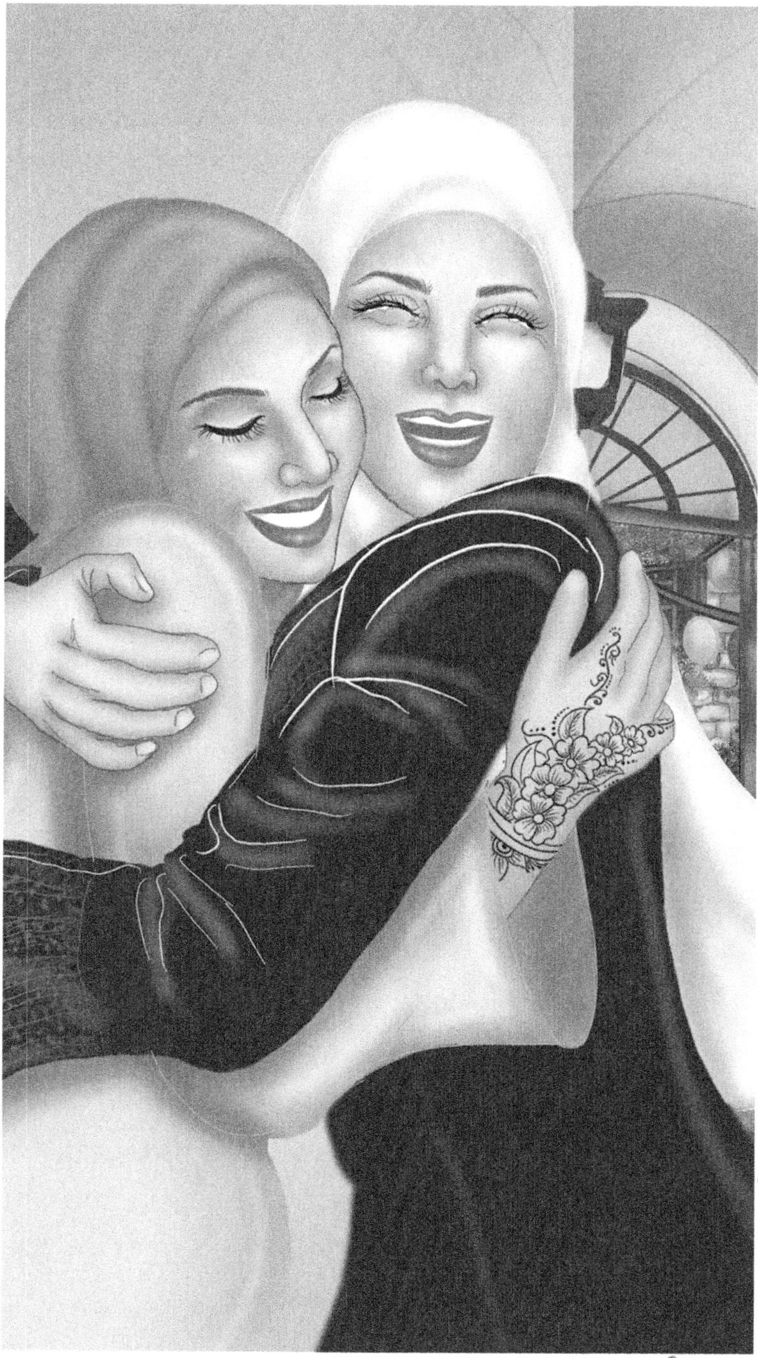

THE SIXTEENTH SCENE

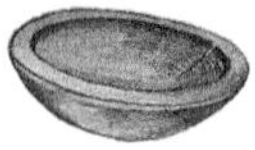

The old house was filled with joy, where elegance embraces originality. On the big wall there was a painting of ancient Haifa and a white dove flying in its sky. On the opposite wall they hanged the map of Palestine and next to it the key of the big city; the owner of the place is the owner of the key, of return and steadfastness.

The family gathered once again, they sat to have their Palestinian delicious breakfast, the aromatic smell of tea with **sage (*known as Maramia*)** prepared by Mohammad, embraced the family's warm talks, their memories and laughter.

THE SEVENTEENTH SCENE

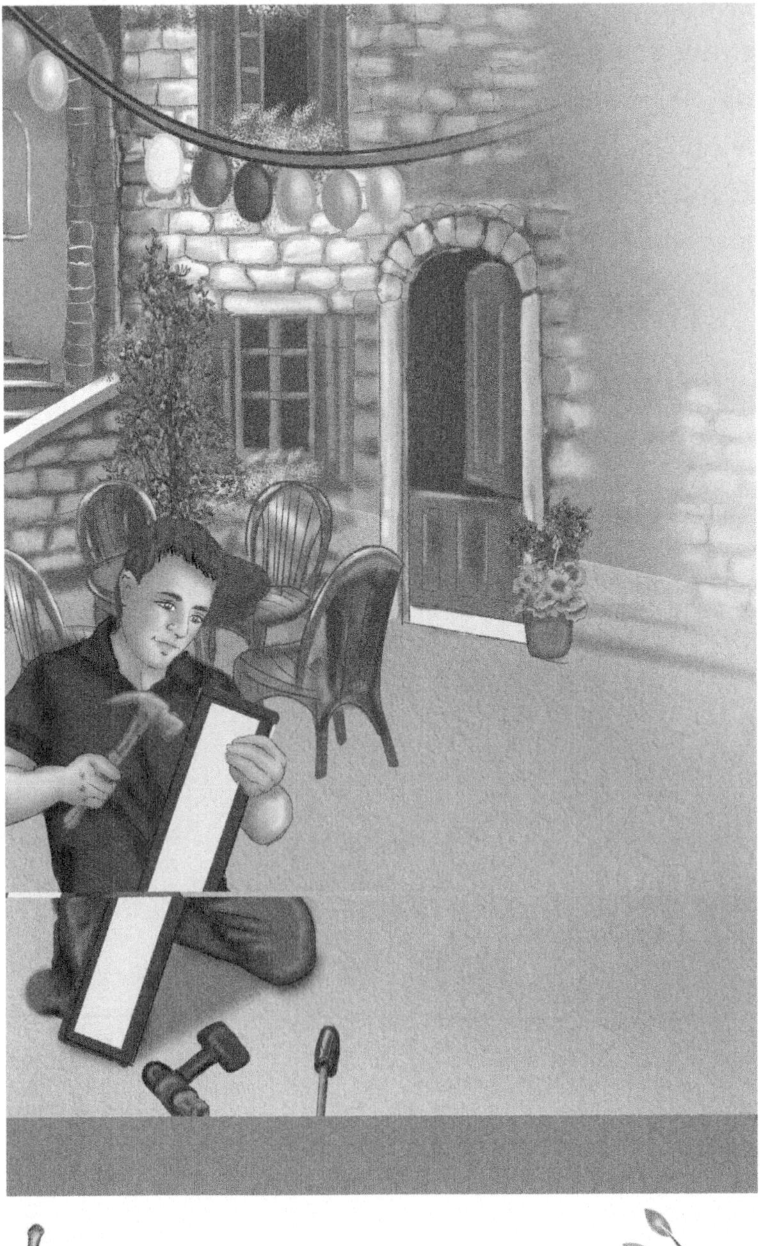

Two weeks have passed since Asmaa had come, she decided to display her paintings in the front yard of her home, some neighbors will participate their paintings too, they will bring their paintings with the topic related to the city. Asmaa was a talented journalist besides her drawing talents.

Asmaa published an announcement about her exhibition through social media pages; also she prepared small leaflets talking about it. Hasan distributed them to the close Arab neighborhoods starting with **Wadi Al-Nisnas**, and then **AL Hollaisa, Kababir, Abbas district, Carmel Station** and **Wadi Al Jemal.**

Asmaa's dad and uncle made different frames for the paintings, Mohammad and his friends participated in painting them with various colors.

At dawn, on the day of the exhibition, and as the time accelerates with the energy that began early in the house of Abu Mohammed, Asmaa's parents rushed to the hospital. Asmaa is going to give birth to her new child.

Mohammad: thanks God, Asmaa has delivered a beautiful baby girl. Hopefully she can come in the evening and we'll take care of everything.

Hasan: will many people attend?

Mohammad: I think so; the people of Haifa are keen to attend those exhibitions that support their steadfastness within the city.

Hasan: I prepared a special painting; put it in a remarkable place please.

Mohammad: I know, your painting will be hanged in the entrance at the main gate, Asmaa undoubtedly will love it.

Hasan: If all the paintings are sold, we will contribute in building the Arab school as people of the neighborhood earlier made a deal. The whole world will see Haifa with its Palestinian aspirations.

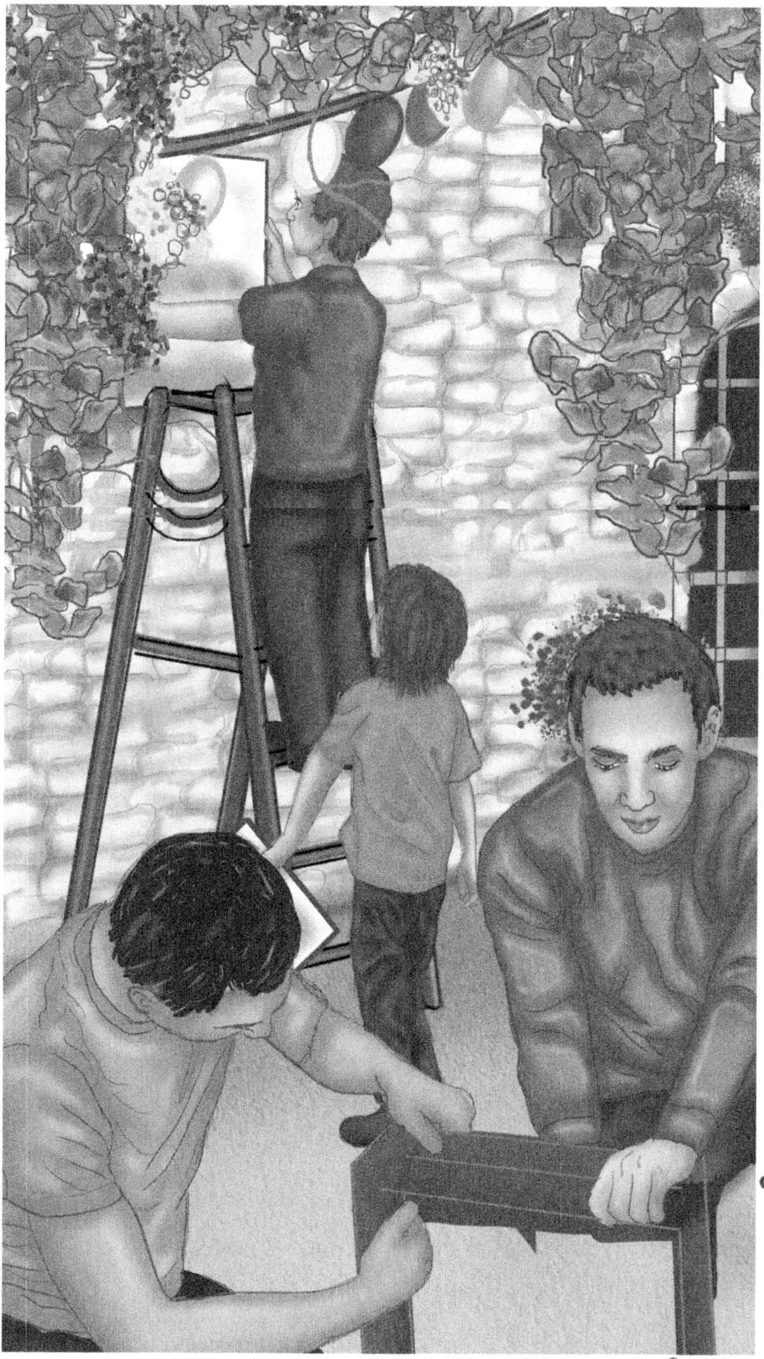

THE EIGHTEENTH SCENE

انا
حيفا
I
HAIFA
انا
حيفا
I
HAIFA

The front yard was full of attendants from all over theneighborhoods.

The fragment

I LOVE Haifa

printed in white font on the youth's black T-shirts symbolized the clarity of the truth even with the intensification of injustice and darkness. Everyone seemed impressed with the paintings fore fronted by a large painting about the lives of people in the past, and another painting about a giant

oak tree in ***Wadi Al-Nisnas*** shading on the small cottages. A painting embodies the beautiful beach surrounding the shiny golden waters.

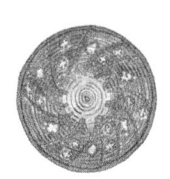

Rochmeia Bridge with its special arches was the main subject adults talked about in memorizing their childhood, and how mujahideen (fighters) resisted the occupiers. It was the largest bridge in Palestine at the time; it connected the neighborhoods and facilitated movement between them.

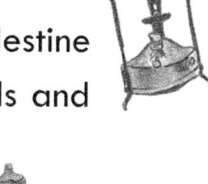

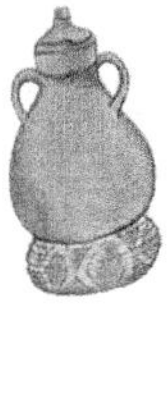

THE NINETEENTH SCENE

With hard work we reach our goals
انا
حيفا
I
HAIFA

Its evening now, Asmaa didn't come yet. Hasan with tearful eyes and disappointment sneaking into his small heart sat squatting and asked God not to disappoint him.

Suddenly he heard Asmaa's voice calling him joyfully after she revealed the cover of the painting.

Its frame was made with colored shells, in the middle he drew the view of the mountain on the sea with small seashells and colored sand. His painting appeared as if it is a three dimension painting.

He wrote on each shell a letter of the following phrase:

With hard work we reach our goals

Asmaa: Hasan, you are an artist! Did you draw it brother? It is a piece of art, I can't believe, this is Haifa, and this is the great hope and love that always inhabits us.

Hasan: thanks God you are safe, I'm glad you were able to come at the end. Where is the baby? What did you name her?

Asmaa: I was hesitant, but now the name has become a sure fact,

I named her Amal (hope) Haifa, our hope!

The grandmother finished her beautiful story of Haifa, her grandchildren around her surrendered to sleep with drowsy eyes.

Everything outside went calm. Even the fresh breeze. She covered their slim bodies with a blanket.

HoPeNworK

and more...

Lessons learned from the story of Haifa

انا ♥ حيفا
I ♥ HAIFA
انا ♥ حيفا
I ♥ HAIFA

Patriotism is part of faith, with knowledge we build our homeland, working for it and defending it from invaders is legislated by all fair laws and religions.

The Palestinian family has proven throughout the ages, and everywhere, that it is an authentic family; strong and cohesive, proud of its heritage and customs, and protects its origins and roots, upholds its identity and never leaves its right. Its residents perform their role with dedication towards their families, homeland and society.

The people of Wadi Al-Nisnas and the Arab neighborhoods of Haifa have been a brave example of the steadfastness in front of the Zionist occupation, despite the difficult circumstances the occupation had put against them by enacting unjust laws, changing the names of the old city's landmarks or changing the curriculum from Arabic to Hebrew.

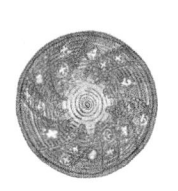

The Palestinian people are keen to establish their full identity and right in Palestine through organizing various events inside and outside Palestine, and to invest its profit in the reconstruction of neighborhoods, places and holy sites that have been closed or destroyed by the occupation.

Questions about the story of Haifa

The first scene
- How did Hasan help his family?

The second scene
- Why did Hasan's grandfather meet with the neighborhood's men?

The third scene
- What was Hasan's mom making in her Palestinian kitchen in the morning?
- Have you ever tasted Palestinian manakish? Do you know its ingredients?
- For what do Palestinians use the "Saj"?

The fourth scene
- What is the name of the neighborhood where Hasan and his family live?
- Write two pieces of information about Wadi al-Nisnas mentioned in the story?
- What's the reason behind giving Wadi al-nisnas this name?

The fifth scene
- What was the surprise that Hasan hid in the Carmel bushes?
- What does Hasan do in the Mount Carmel with his grandfather? Why?
- What is the name of the newspaper in which the grandfather published his articles, and which was the first newspaper to warn of the danger of Zionist migrations to Palestine?

The sixth scene
- Why did the grandpa call Haifa (the beautiful past)?
Mention some of the occupations and businesses that the people of Haifa worked in.
- Mention two of Haifa's landmarks.

The seventh scene
- What's the name of the first Palestinian ruler who built modern Haifa, can you describe the building?
- What did sheik zaher al-omar do to develop the city of Haifa?

The eighth scene
- Mention the smart idea Haifa's people suggested in the reopening of the Grand Nasser Mosque which was called Aljuraina, after the Zionist occupation closed it?
- What is the clock tower, as mentioned in the story? In which era was it built?

The ninth scene
- Why was Mount Carmel given this name? What does this beautiful name mean?
- What is the name of the sea on which Haifa has its view?
- What's the name of the beautiful flower that gives Haifa its stunning beauty?

The tenth scene
- What does Hakoora mean?

The eleventh scene
- In what did Hasan help his mom when they were in Asmaa's room?
- Who is the hero leader who liberated Palestine from the hands of the Crusaders in the famous battle «Hittin»?

The twelfth scene
- What does Palestinian Nakba mean?
- Who is the Haganah army? What was their role in the city of Haifa?
- What did the Zionist occupation steal after forcing people to leave their homes and leave through the port?
- What was Hasan's wish when growing up?

The thirteenth scene
- What flourished Haifa before the occupation of the Zionists?
- How did Sultan Abdul Hamid II connect Haifa with the other neighboring cities?

The fourteenth scene
- Describe the parent's joy when their daughter Asmaa' returned from foreign lands.

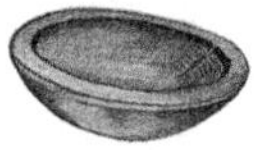

The fifteenth scene
- What did Hasan's family hang on the walls of their house?

The sixteenth scene
- How did Asmaa' announce her exhibition that was going to be held in the front yard of her house?
- How did Hasan help his sister in the exhibition announcement?

The seventeenth scene
- How did Hasan's family serve their country through their exhibition?

The eighteenth scene
- What was the patriotic phrase written on the youth's black shirts?

- What is the Rochmeia Bridge? And why it was the main memory talk of adults in their childhood and of the Mujahideen too?

The nineteenth scene
- Describe the surprise Hasan made for his sister, what did he write on it?
- What was the name Asmaa' gave for her daughter?

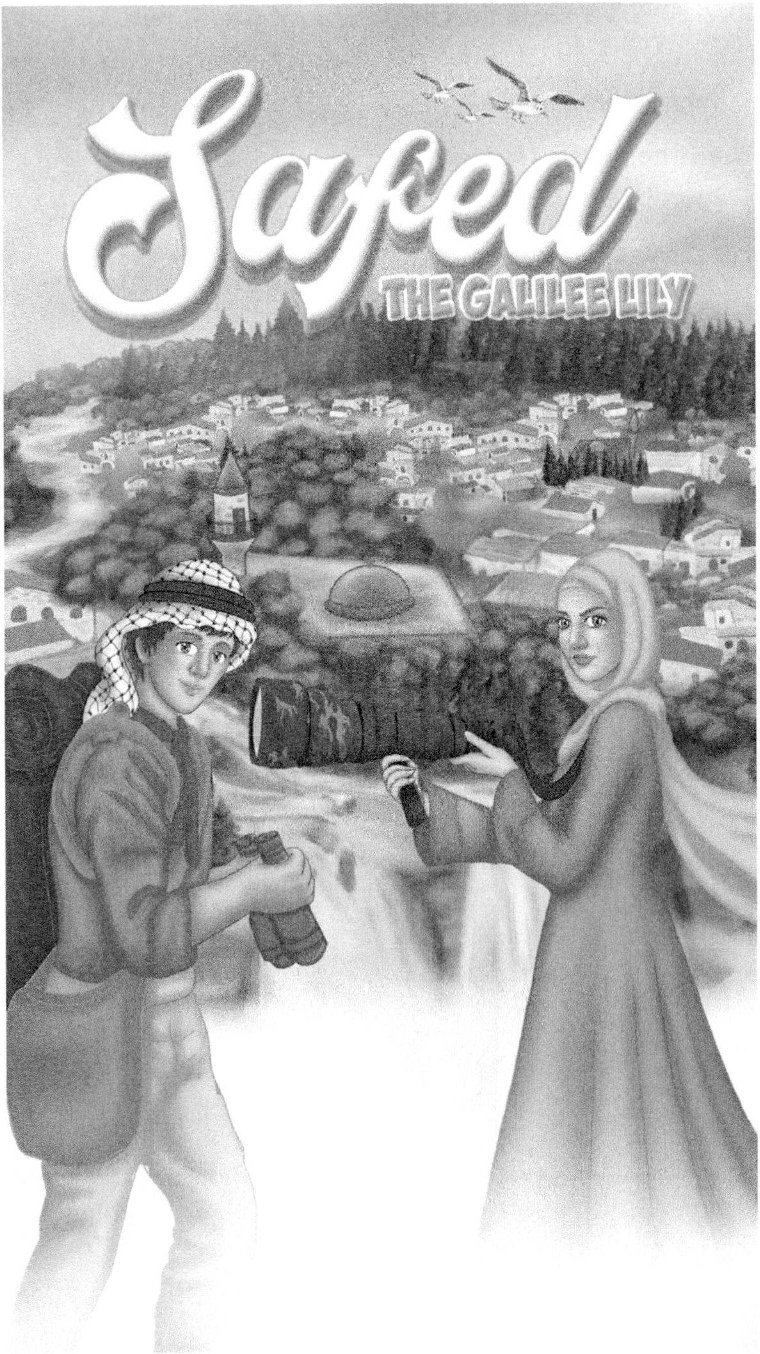
Safed
THE GALILEE LILY

SAFED
THE GALILEE LILY

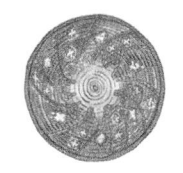

The grandmother entered accompanied with her grandchildren singing a beautiful song about Palestine:

Ouf Ouf Ouf Yaba
my country of olive
almonds and lemon blossoms
we're done with being far away
we missed the windflowers..

Children shouted: wow!

Its evening now, children gathered in an instant, its story time, their grandma promised to tell them a story about Safed. She was very nostalgic, surprisingly Raja'a made a painting. That is fantastic! There was a challenge between her and her brothers, that's why she prepared her colors. She has to finish her paintings in two days instead of three; her paintings were about nature, birds, rivers and a tree.

Grandma: My creative grandchildren, challenge has many types, the people of Safed have faced lots of hard challenges. Our story today is about Safed and one of the challenges they underwent; the return camp, its calls and chants that revived souls, and remind people of the right of return and their duties towards their country.

She stared to tell them the story of Abu Ahmad Al-nahawi, a man so proud, his face was full of wrinkles but in his heart faith speaks so loud. He is one of Safed's sons. The city of fresh breeze, hearts as pure as gold and a beautiful nature. The children came closer to her, when they noticed her glamorous eyes, and emotional voice growing louder. She told them the story of steadfastness of Safed and its people, their determination and their survival. Those who were forced to abandon but couldn't forget the beauty of Safed. They swore to God that they will return and injustice will vanish even if it is prolonged.

THE FIRST SCENE

Sheikh Abu Ahmed al-Nahawi sat on a short wooden bench holding a long, dry branch. This eighty years man was staring at the ground as he draws a map on the dirt, he was one of the first of Mujahideen (fighters) of Safed, the Zionists occupied his house and expelled him and his large family after a great struggling story.

A large number of Scout teams and their leaders stood in front of him, dominated by silence brought by the emotional situation and memories, perhaps the thrill rose because of the lines the old man drew on the ground in front of them, he added some circles to his drawing, murmuring:

(We will never quit, I know that today is followed by tomorrow, my brain and heart are there for jihad (war). I'll never slant, never get bored, and never dawdle).

The old man raised his head, to find out that the number of visitors and guests to the camp is increasing steadily; each of them has taken his place between the audience around the fire lit in the middle, its glow was shining, and light is reflecting on the wrinkles of the face and eyes of the old man which were filled with events, stories and experiences of years' conquering.

The sound of creaky burning wood filled up the place when suddenly it was cut off by the husky man's voice.

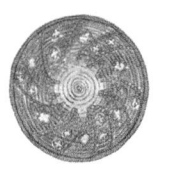

THE SECOND SCENE

Abu Ahmad: my sons and daughters, I wish you could hear my heart beats; it beats with love to Safed's beautiful nature and springs. Safed, my dears, is God's paradise in earth. Its precious vineyards carrying numerous clusters, the huge almond, pine and figs trees, the oaks extending shades and aroma, filling the places with the smell of refreshing nature, olive trees with its distinctive green color and citrus trees, and its incomparable blossoms, peach trees and pears, which send love and welfare to all, its air is refreshing, its residents are authentic gold, The beauty of its nature is unparalleled.

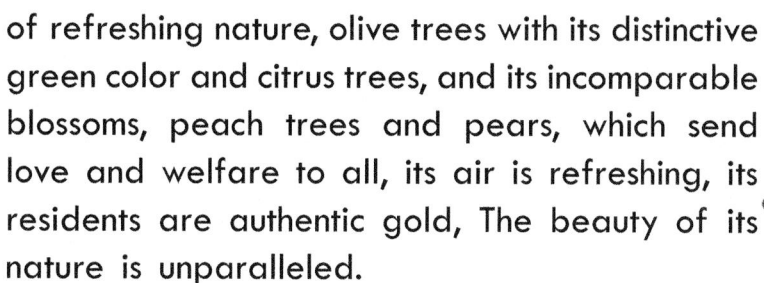

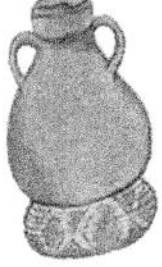

THE THIRD SCENE

Scout boy Kanaan: uncle, what a suspense! Your description is beyond imagination. We are curious to know more about Safed and the secret lines and circles you drew on the ground.

Abu Ahmad: Safed, my son, means a fortified fortress. Its former name was Safat which means cover and bond. It is "bond" according to me,

it was constrained and hard to be reached by invaders being isolated and surrounded by mountains. He pointed to the earth saying: These lines are the map of Safed and its location. It is located in **the Upper Galilee** region and is viewed by **Mount Meron (Jarmaq)** the highest mountain in Palestine, also Safed hill has a view on al-Hula

charming plain with its beautiful rivers, green plants, generous springs and welfare.

Safed my sons, is located on a very old mountain, do you know its name?

Hiba: I think that its name is Mount Canaan, in a relation to Canaanites of Arabia who were responsible of building it in ancient times.

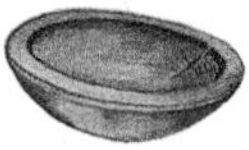

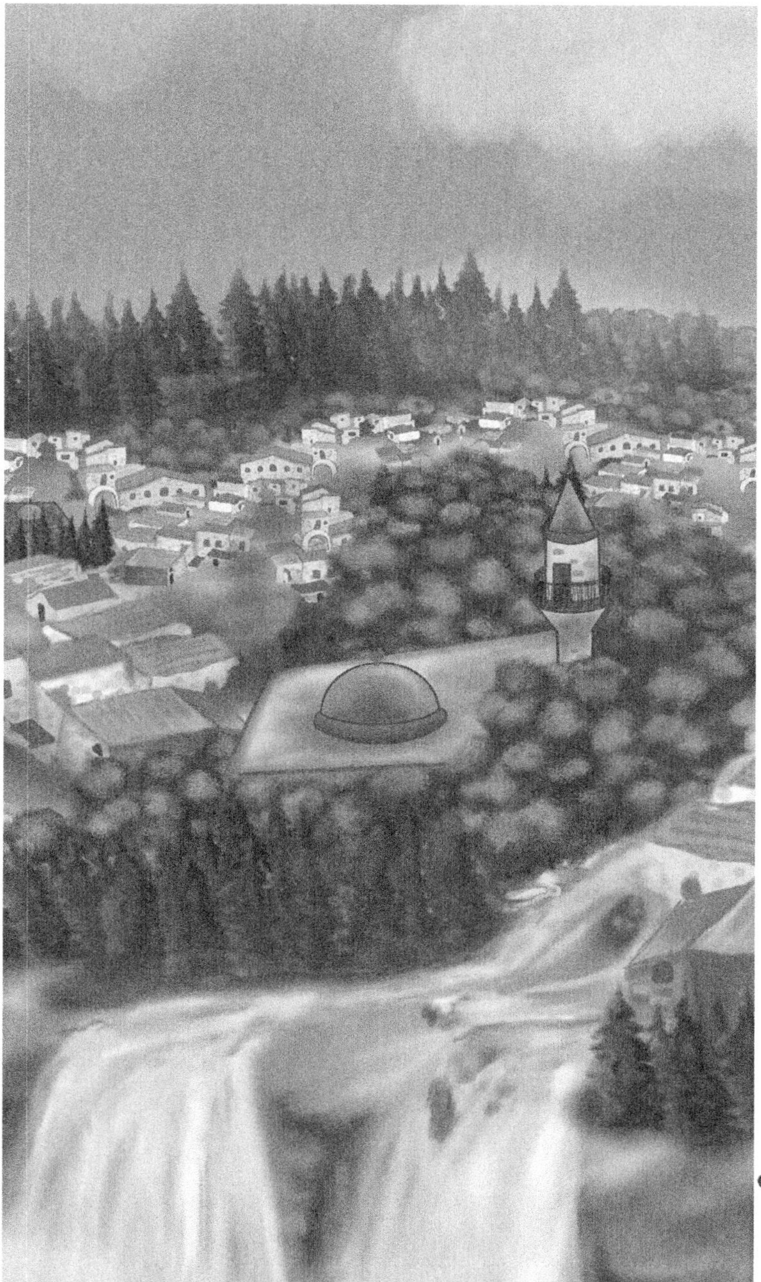
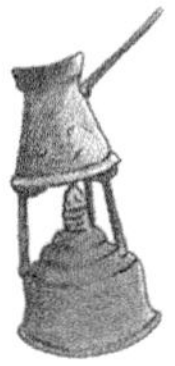
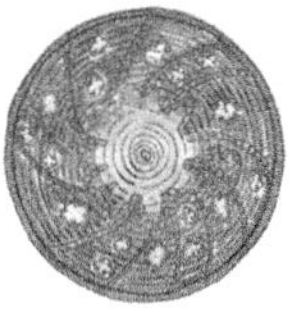
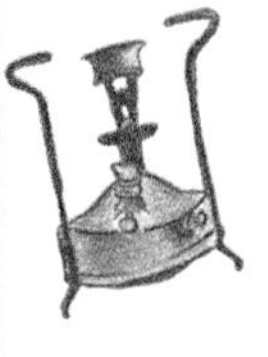
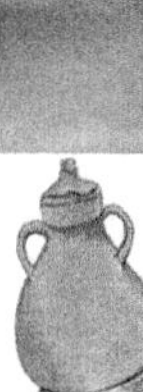

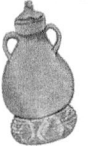

THE FOURTH SCENE

Abu Ahmad: yes, well done my daughter. The beautiful houses of Safed were closely linked, and the roads were mostly a series of steps, its entrances were decorated with beautiful arches connecting the neighborhoods together, so the viewer feels astonished.

Safed's people are very generous, stuck to their traditions, and predominated by Islamic character.

They lived side-by-side, loving, sharing and standing by each other's in happiness and sorrows. People there are endowed with loving hearts and giving souls, exactly like the soil of their homeland.

THE FIFTH SCENE

Ayat couldn't resist her curiosity to know more so she asked: how did the Jews enter Safed? And why they were able to live inside between its residents?

Abu Ahmad: The people of Safed were generous and helping, they welcomed every immigrant to their city from neighboring areas or even distant ones. Among these immigrants were the "Jews" who had settled in a little quarter, we used to call the "***Jewish Quarter***", we did not know that they had a sabotage intent to occupy our country , and that betrayal to those who embraced them when they were seeking asylum was part of their character and their purpose from the beginning.

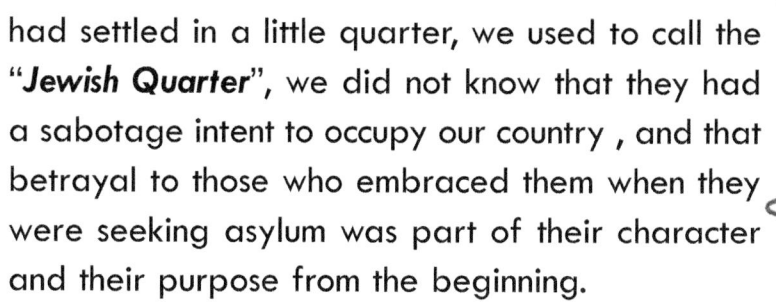

Unlike our beloved people of **Algeria** and **Morocco**

who were forced to immigrate to Safed, and with time passing and the hospitality they found, the differences between them started to melt and they merged among the people of the city and became part of them, never forgetting their virtue and generosity.

103

THE SIXTH SCENE

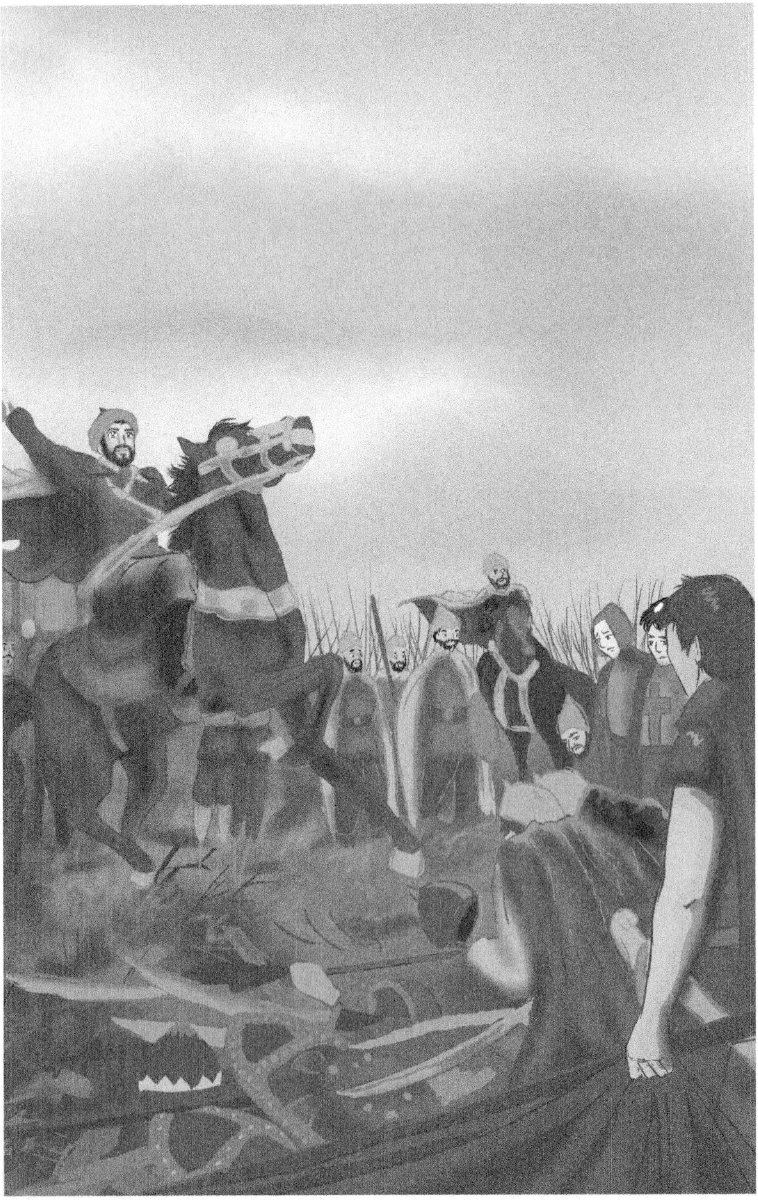

Abu Ahmad continued his talk pointing to the map: And this is the famous fortress of Safed, built by the Crusaders when they occupied our country. And liberated by the commander (**Salah al-Din al–Ayyubi**) who also liberated a lot of Palestinian cities in the famous battle «**Hittin**», but the Crusaders then reoccupied them again, then arrived **Al-Zaher Beybars** and liberated them once again. He established justice there and built a mosque with a school of science in his name.

Hanin: the greed of the invaders must be for an important reason, isn't that true uncle?

Abu Ahmad: of course my daughter. Its geographical importance which I formerly told you about and its natural resources were sufficient reasons for invaders and rapists.

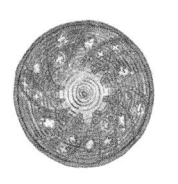

THE SEVENTH SCENE

Over the ages, Safed has enjoyed the prosperity of trade, where residents and traders came from cities and close areas to sell and purchase, its people worked in textile fabric of all kinds. During the Mamluk era they were known of silk weaving and exporting it to Europe, Also they were famous for exporting cotton, rice and soap.

It was a postal station between Syria and Egypt, letters were delivered by pigeons.

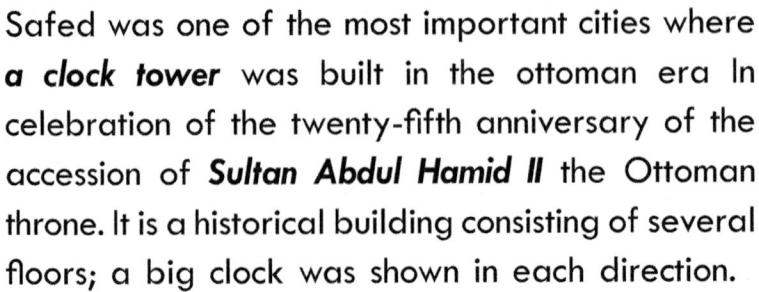

Safed was one of the most important cities where **a clock tower** was built in the ottoman era In celebration of the twenty-fifth anniversary of the accession of **Sultan Abdul Hamid II** the Ottoman throne. It is a historical building consisting of several floors; a big clock was shown in each direction.

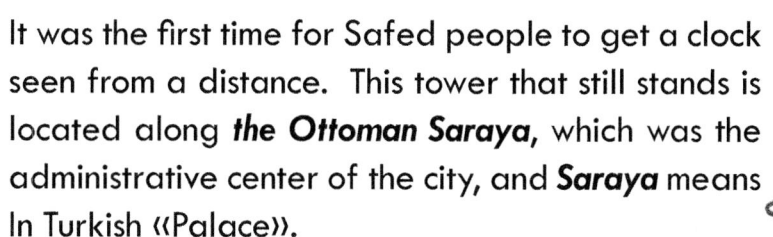

It was the first time for Safed people to get a clock seen from a distance. This tower that still stands is located along **the Ottoman Saraya**, which was the administrative center of the city, and **Saraya** means In Turkish «Palace».

THE EIGHTH SCENE

FUKA'EYYEH
ZANJAL
TABE' BREAD
EID CAKES
MA'AMOUL
TAHINI
SAFEDI KUNAFA
AWWAMA
BGHARIEH
MUSHABBAK

Hanin: what about Safed's famous foods and traditional plates, uncle?

Abu Ahmad: our beloved city was famous of its delicious and traditional dishes, he started to count them with a smile over his face:

Jozyeh (walnut cookies), ***tahini*** (sesame sauce),

mushabbak (fried dough), *awwama* (sweet dumplings), the famous **Safedi kunafa** (toasted vermicelli with white cheese), *ma'amoul* (dates cookies), *barazek* (sesame cookies), **Bughariyya** (A crunchy, pie-like circular dough served with honey, sugar, cream or walnuts) And the famous **Tabe' bread** (yellow spiced bread).

He continued: oh my god how delicious is the meat stuffed **Zanjal** (stuffed and fried salty pies) and *fuka'eyyeh* (rice, beans and yoghurt pudding).

The voices of girls and women began to rise; they were impressed by the precise information and the vast knowledge of this old man, and his accuracy in mentioning the Safed dishes by its old names.

Abu Ahmad: shall I complete or stop mentioning the dishes?

The women answered with one loud voice, no, no, continue please (The camp was filled with laughter and applause).

Abu Ahmad headed towards them with a question testing their feminine culture.

Abu Ahmad: Who can tell us what the women of Safed used to wear, and what was their main characteristic that differentiates them from the rest of women?

Abeer: Safed's women, what do you know about women of Safed! The sisters of men (a proverb used to describe brave women).

They used to wear **Melaya** over their elegant clothes, which reflected art and taste having brilliant golden color Interspersed with those black, thin threads as the rays of the dawn shining on the darkness, and drawing joy and hope, and growing Pleasure in the eyes.

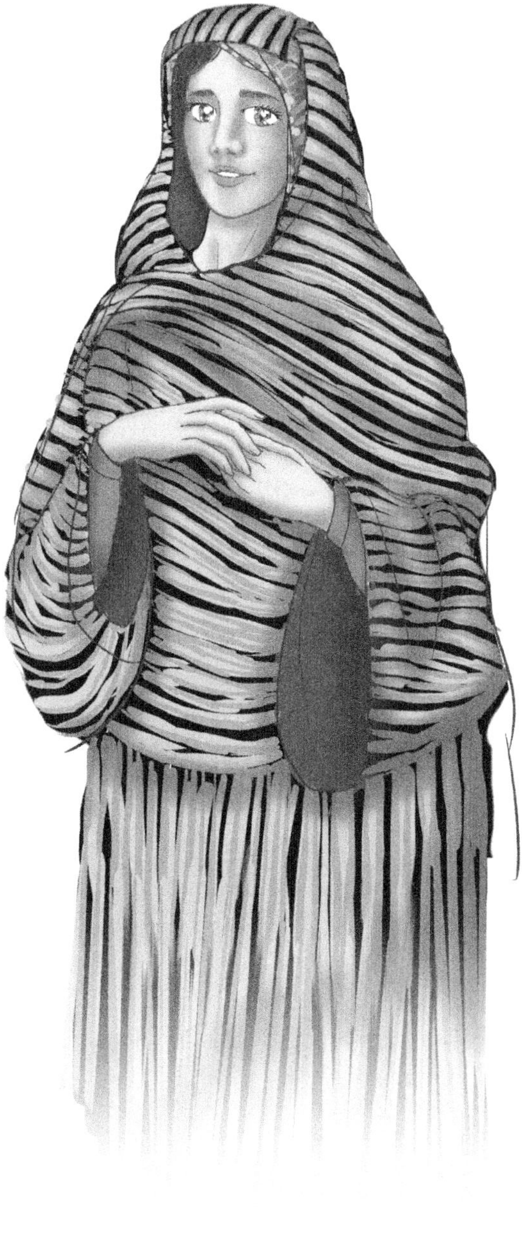
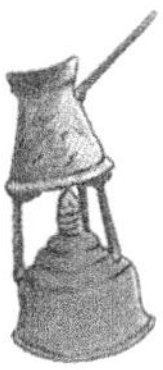
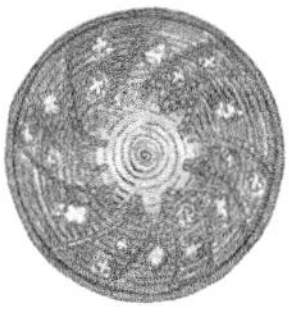
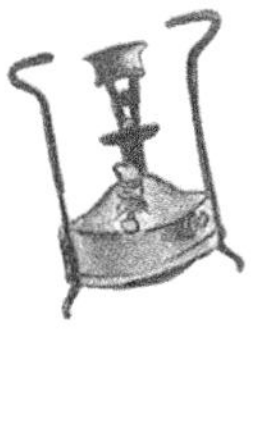
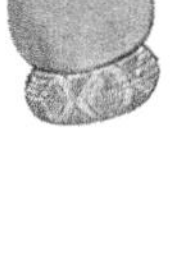

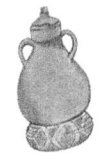

THE NINTH SCENE

Salah: My uncle Abu Ahmed, your eyes tell a lot, is it a longing for the past, or Sadness because of it??

Silence dominated once again, all the eyes followed the old man. His eyes are surrounded by a glint of defiance, but conceal a deep sadness in his face; he had thick eyebrows as if they were guardians.

Abu Ahmed: I am saddened, my son, seeing roads and valleys inhabited by the extremist outsiders.

I'm saddened for the Safed mosques. The occupation destroyed part of them and tampered the rest.

I am saddened for **the Red Mosque** built by **al-Zaher Baybars** in the Mamluk era and now is used for everything but prayers.

I'm saddened for the (**Yunesi**) Market Mosque, which was established in **Sultan Abdulhamid II** era and the occupation changed it into a museum for pictures and sculptures.

I'm saddened for the **Swaiqa Mosque**; it is totally destroyed, nothing remained from it except the minaret to be a witness for what the occupation has done.

Even **the Roman Orthodox Church**, the only one in the city of Safed, did not escape the harm of the occupation, turning it into a museum of pictures and statues.

Omar: Why do the Zionists insult and humiliate Islamic and Christian sanctities and destroy them, while they could just close them or practice their worship instead? Allah says (interpretation of the meaning): "And who can be more unjust than those who prohibit the name of Allah from being remembered in any of His houses of worship and strive to ruin them?"

Abu Ahmed: God the almighty has spoken the truth, listen my son, the Zionists have made laws that oblige them to use everything that is not decent or morally accepted in an attempt to break the Palestinian will and provoke them, and what they do by desecrating the holy places in an attempt to hurt Muslims feelings since these holy places has a big effect on their lives, and a big place in their heart

THE TENTH SCENE

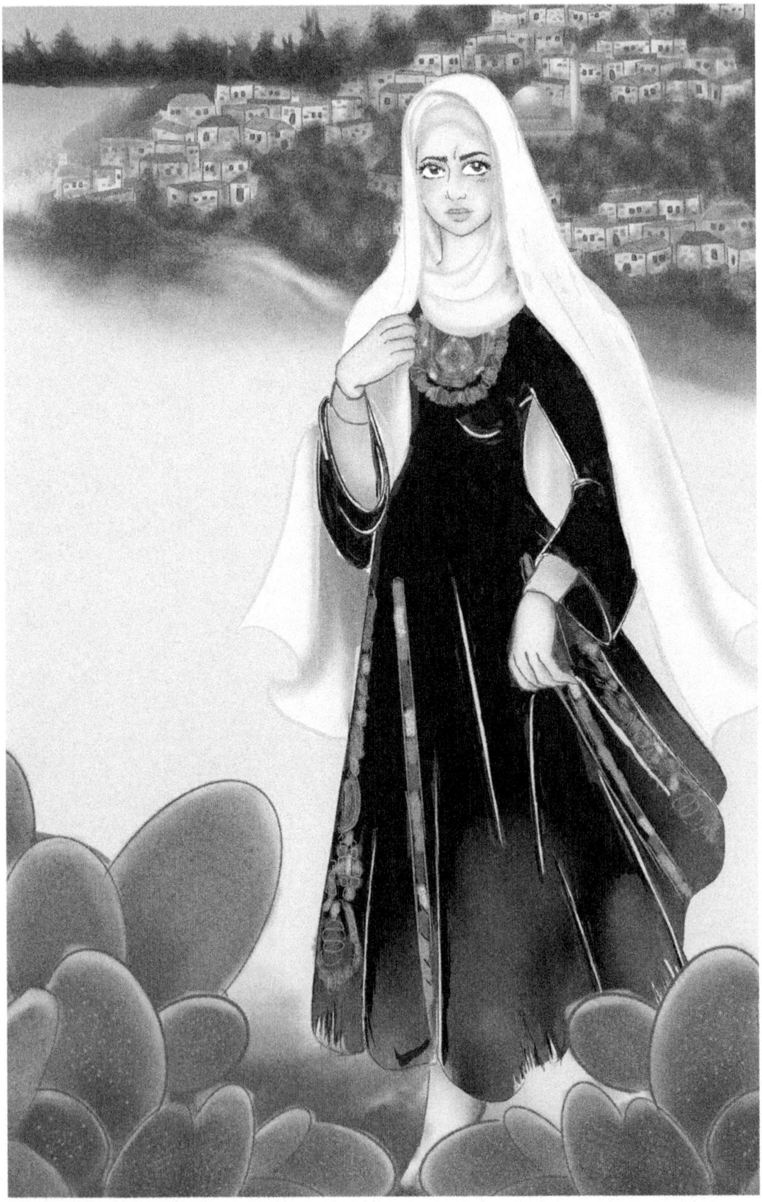

Amer (astonished) and provoked by the Sheikh's talk about the confiscation of **Zionists** to the mosques of Safed: Why the Mujahideen handed Safed that easy, uncle!

Abu Ahmad: They did not do so, son, read history well, you will know that the people of Palestine do not betray Or surrender, whatever the case is.

I was at the age of 20 when we faced the well trained gangs of **Zionist Haganah**, we defended our beloved city bravely, and even defeated them on more than one tour, and many young people were killed from our city and its neighboring cities.

There was a shortage in supplies, my son, as well as the strength of the enemy and the large military forces, they also received help from the British colonialism who was occupying our country at that time, forcing the Mujahideen to withdraw, and Safed and its villages fell one by one in the hands of the enemy.

I still remember our neighbor Abu Muwaffaq, how was forced to leave with his new bride to Lebanon, and how her shoes were teared but she continued walking barefoot on the thorns of the road without being able to take their needs and belongings, and then they were carried by a

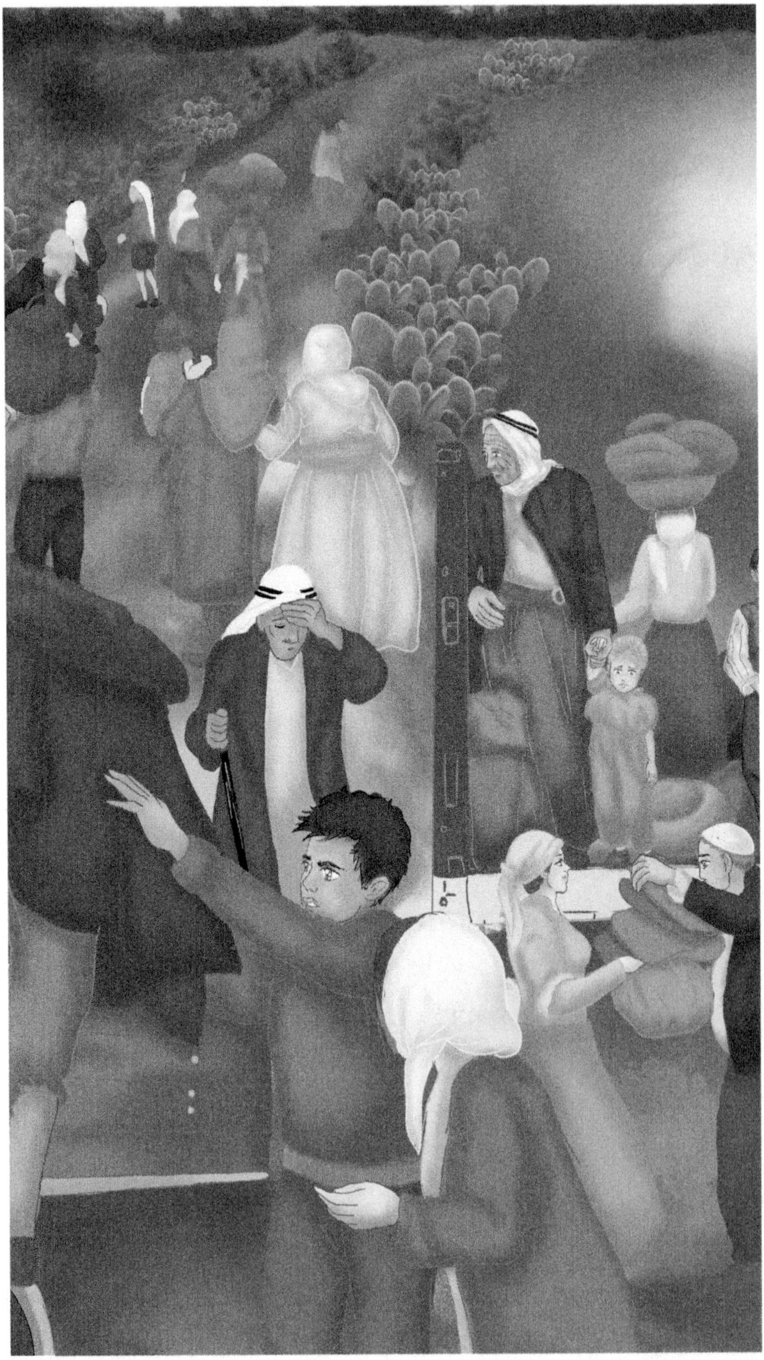

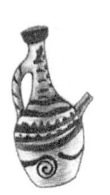

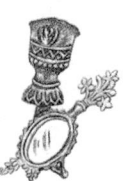

cattle transporting truck to the city of Aleppo in Syria.

His wife hid her tears and bitterness. She looked with all her strength and defiance to the soldiers of the occupation when she left, she looked to the ground and the city then swore she will return no matter how long it takes.

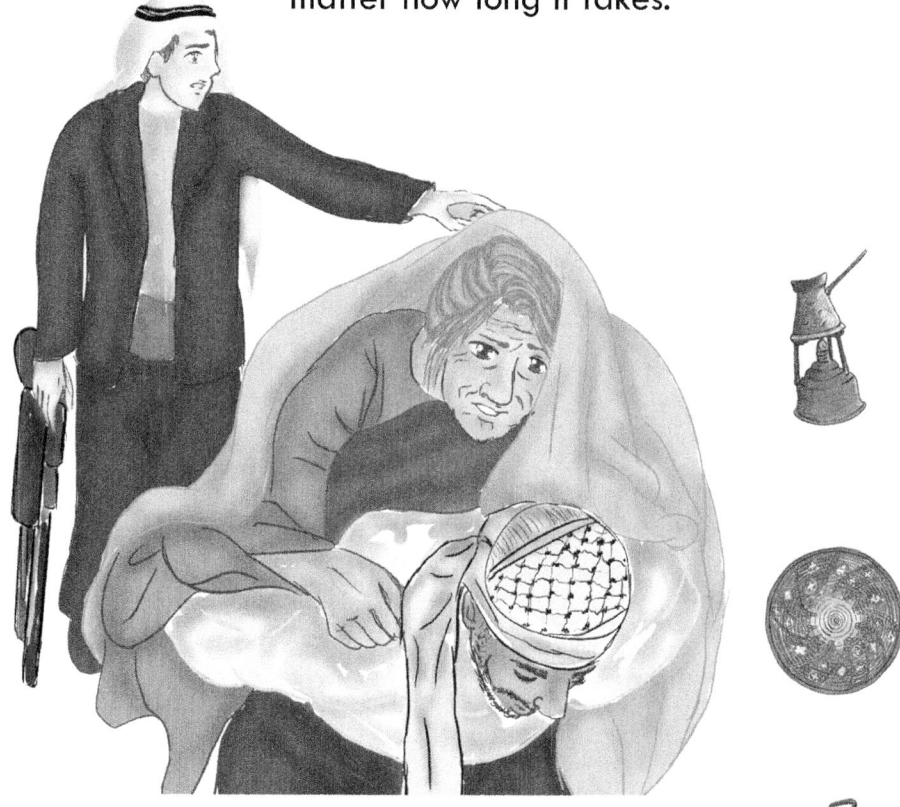

Kanaan: I swear to the land and the city that my right to return won't be forgotten, Safed, the land of the rebels, the land of freedom, standing In the face of all the betraying intruders.

THE ELEVENTH SCENE

Abu Ahmed: Indeed, Safed was the main station for the revolutions of the heroic Palestinian people in the face of colonialism and the resistance of the Zionist enemy and their emigration into Palestine. I was with the Mujahideen wearing the **Hatta** (head cloth designed to protect the wearer from sand and heat) that was a symbol of struggle. We called on the roads «*take of the tarboush, and wear the Hatta, that's what revolution taught us*», in an attempt to encourage people to resist. My hope for your generation, my children, is great, but hope must be supported by action.

Abu Ahmed's granddaughter was studying journalism and media at Safed University College, her struggle is the secret of her survival, and Khulood The granddaughter of Abu Muwaffaq is a documentary filmmaker at one of the major television stations, and she managed through her identity as a journalist to be present on her beloved land, despite the objections of ***the Zionists*** and their hostile treatment of her. She was expelled from her rented home more than once being a Palestinian Arab. Many of those who know her testify that she has a strong will, love for life, and defends oppressed human rights wherever she goes.

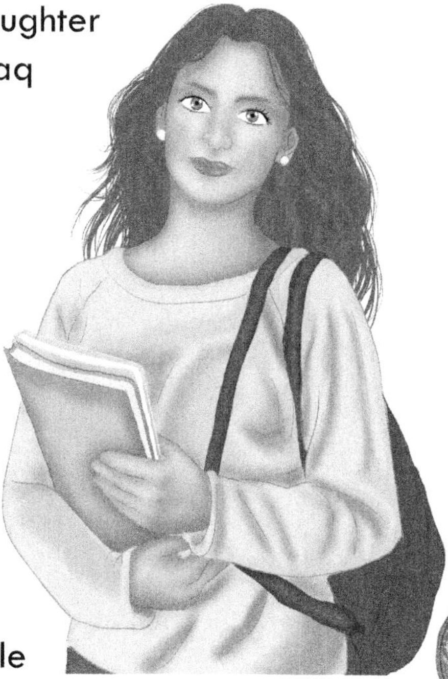

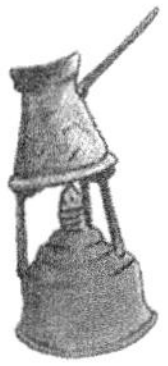

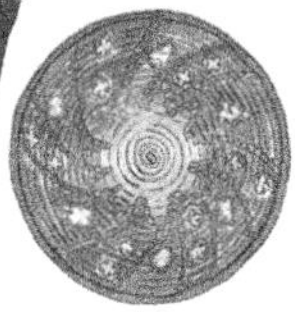

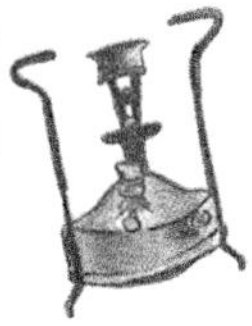

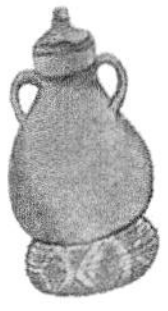

Through her work she documented everything, starting from the occupied Palestinian homes, then the historical monuments and ending with the ruined mosques that **The Zionists** transformed them into barns or celebration yards.

She lived her present and recorded in her lens the charming nature of **Upper Galilee** and the beautiful roads surrounded by plants and flowers, she was obsessed with photographing huge trees that tell the stories of steadfastness to those who planted it.

THE TWELFTH SCENE

A student's voice rose with the call of Isha'a prayer. The girls and women went to their own tents to prepare themselves for prayer while the boys divided into 2 groups, a group went for wudoo' and the other went to extend the large colored mats in the square that mediates the tents.

Sheikh Abu Ahmad noticed a tent lightened from

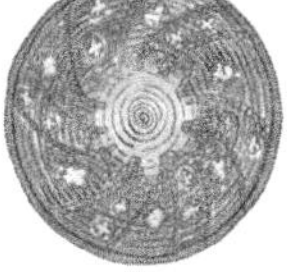

inside all the time, and no one was allowed to enter it, while He finished his wudoo' and sat waiting for the Scouts to start their prayer.

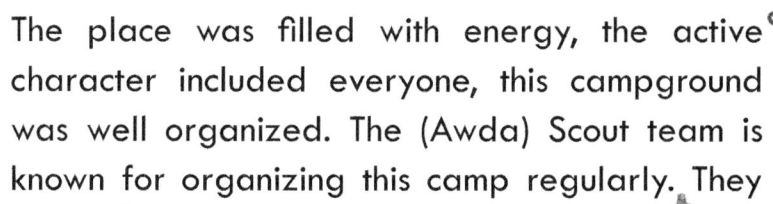

The place was filled with energy, the active character included everyone, this campground was well organized. The (Awda) Scout team is known for organizing this camp regularly. They host the families and dignitaries of the destroyed Palestinian cities and villages to plant hope and remembrance of their right to return back.

The old man was overwhelmed, and felt pride and hope creeping back into his soul, he was glad to see new generations who have never seen their countries before, but full of patriotism, working hard and planning to restore what was stolen from them.

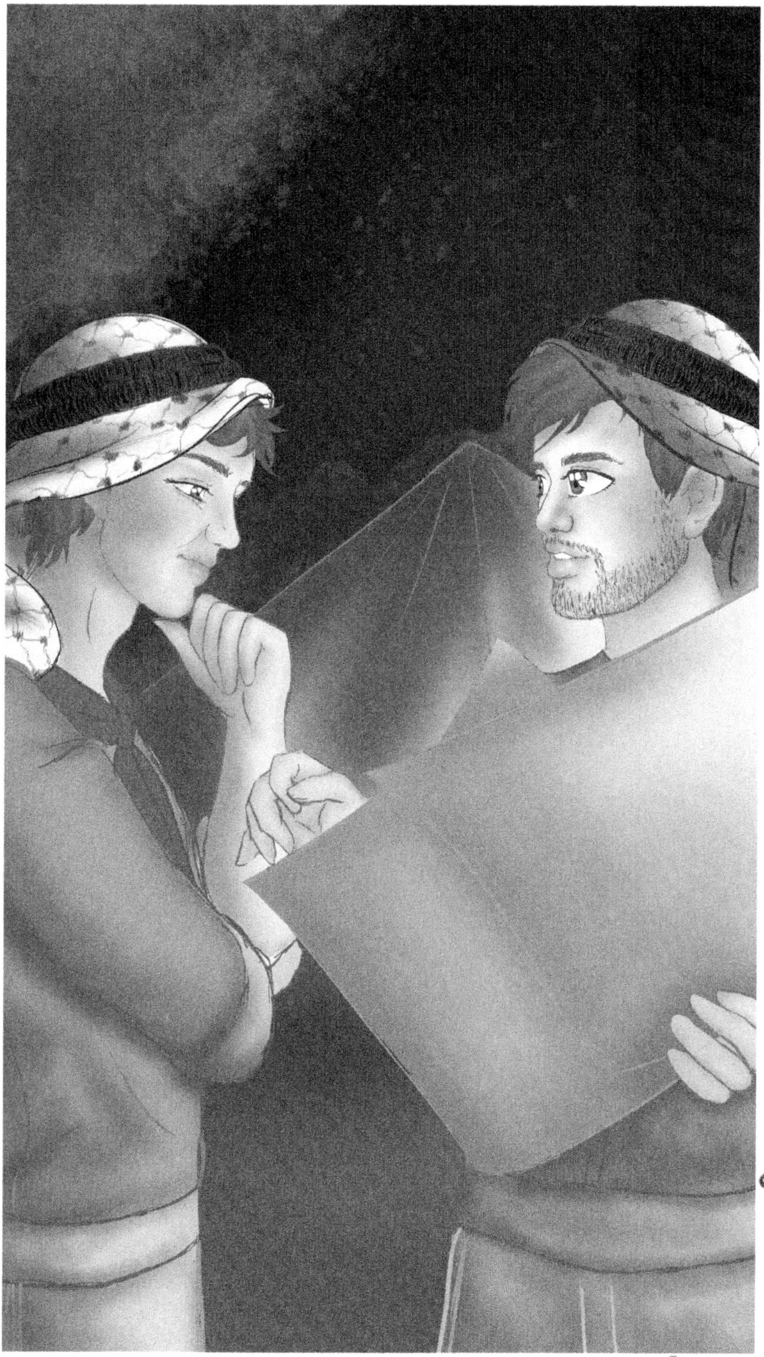

THE THIRTEENTH SCENE

The next morning the old man looked up from the small tent, to find all the Scout teams standing in lines and performing scouting presentations.

The tents were named after the close villages to Safed, **Ein Zeitoun, Akbara, Taheriya, Ja'ouna,** and others. They wrote the names of the neighborhoods on the uniform shirts of the participants, and unintentionally the viewer tries to follow those names, **Al-Sawaween, Al-Joura, Al-Wattah hill**, and the **Kurdish neighborhood**.

The tents were all highly energetic; one of the large tents was prepared in a beautiful heritage, furnished with handmade colored carpets, mediated by a large charcoal grill with Arabic coffee kettles boiling on the top of it, sending its wonderful refreshing aroma.

Some girls took a corner of that tent as a traditional market, an example of what the markets of Safed were, and they sold traditional dishes and some handicrafts of embroidery, pottery and some antiques and souvenirs, while the artists' drawings were hanged on the walls of the tent in a very simple and elegant format, outside the tents, some traditional games were held like hide and seek, hadi badi, and discover the road, where some adults were involved in the games to encourage kids and to bring joy to their hearts.

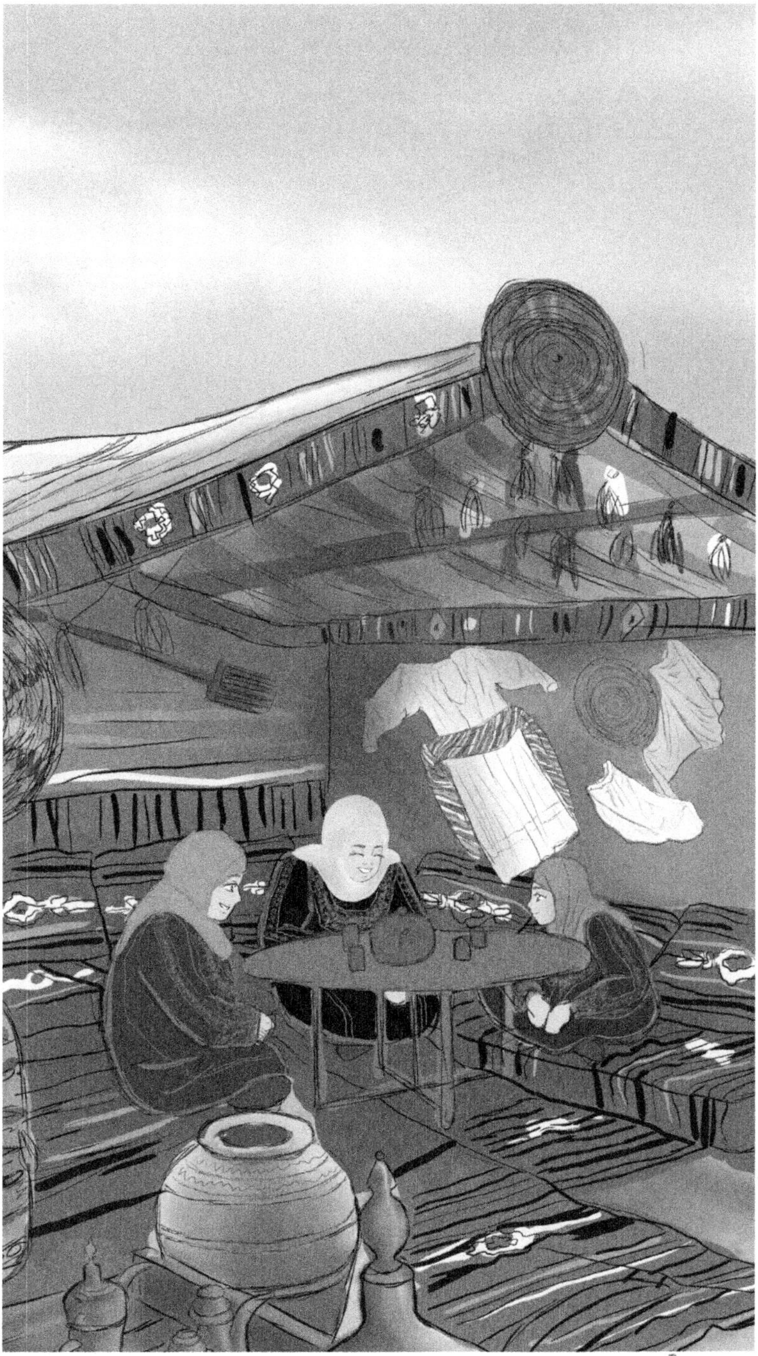
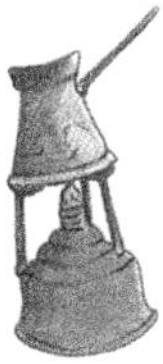
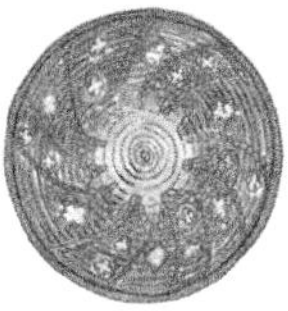
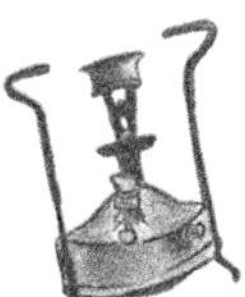
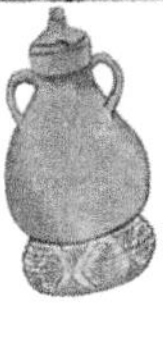

THE FOURTEENTH SCENE

At 3:00 PM, a large car stopped in front of the scout camp and four of the men and a young girl came out, the young girl held on to her old grandfather's hand. Scout's calls and shouts began to sound strong and enthusiastic; everyone looked steady with their right hands on the hearts, followed by powerful *takbirat* (to say Allahu

akbar, which means Allah is the greatest).

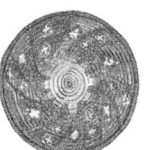

The guests watched the cheers and scouts performance, as they began to hit the ground with their feet making heavy dust, then in a few steps they formed two opposite rows leading to the special tent.

The guests walked between them with glances of approval, along with some important people who were invited, until they reached the door of the tent to find Abu Ahmed al-Nahawi cheering with his strong distinctive voice.

Abu Ahmed: Welcome my brother and best friend Fouad Hijazi (Abu Muwaffaq), what a pleasant surprise! Praise be to God who gathered us after all these years.

Abu Muwaffaq: welcome my jihad companion, my life neighbor, let me hug you my brother.

The two men hugged each other and patted each other's shoulders. Then they started to recall their old memories.

THE FIFTEENTH SCENE

The two men entered with the rest of the guests and a group of important people, followed by the Scouts, all standing inside the big tent waiting to see what was hidden inside for ten days.

The curtain was removed!

And here is a surprise! a large mosque with

138

four large minarets, and a large dome with four small domes surrounding it, accompanied by an institute for Islamic sciences, a cultural center and a library, on the mosque's door was written (**the Galilee's lily mosque**).

The lights from the inside of the object lit reflecting a real mosque, full of worshipers, and the overall landscape was magnified by the real features of Safed surrounding the sides of the tent with large three-dimensional images lit from behind.

Everyone felt that they were there, in the middle of Safed; the city was in front of them, with its beautiful majestic mosque.

Then tears ran out through people's eyes, and the voices of admiration and takbeer rose, when Abu Muwaffaq and his granddaughter Khulood announced that they have collected, with the help of generous people, enough money to support the construction of this whole mosque.

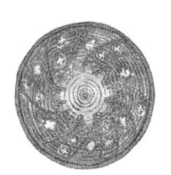

The voice of takbeer increased with great joy. Everyone applauded knowing that this project would be implemented in many Palestinian cities.

Abu Ahmad: Thanks God your generation knew the value of building mosques, even if they (**The Zionists**)

insulted, destroyed or silenced a mosque, we will place ten instead!

Abu Muwaffaq: I had a dream the previous night that a strong earthquake struck Safed again, and the ground broke and emerged from inside a large mosque like this, and I saw **the Zionists** running with fear like rats.

Abu Ahmad: victory is close! Victory is close! Allah is the greatest.. Allah is the greatest.

Everyone raised their voices with takbeer many times, and the enthusiastic and patriotic chants started shaking the place again. O occupier in our country you'll never get bread again, the minarets will build for the Muslims glory and attribute, and with science and work we'll establish a definite victory for us and win.

The grandmother ended her story glorifying her Lord, and laid down close to her grandchildren, and closed her eyes to dream of beautiful Palestine, praying on the Prophet with noble deeds, and ask forgiveness from Allah and thank him for His great blessings.

and more...

Lessons Learned from the story of Safed

Patriotism is part of faith, with knowledge we build our homeland, working for it and defending it from invaders is legislated by all fair laws and religions.

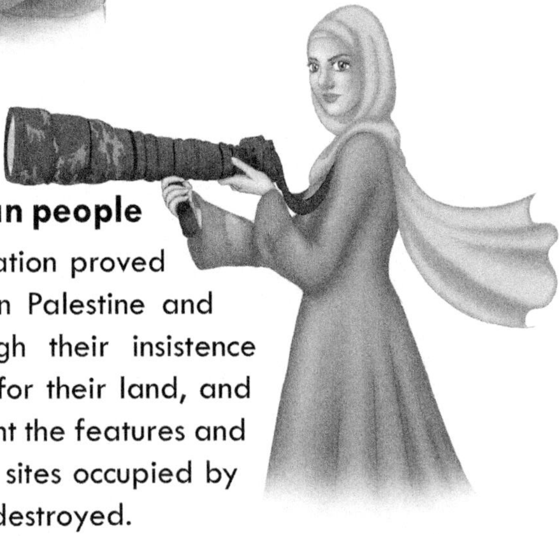

The Palestinian people after the occupation proved their full right in Palestine and its cities, through their insistence on being there for their land, and work to document the features and homes and holy sites occupied by the Zionists or destroyed.

The conquerors who settled in Safed were keen to respect its people, to spread justice among the people and to build the city, and protect the features of their civilization and heritage, while the occupiers spread discrimination and injustice among the people, destroyed the city, displaced its people and insulted their sanctities.

Palestinian refugees in the diaspora have established their identity and their right to return to their homes by setting up camps and various activities and investing their profit for the benefit of their homeland and people.

The Palestinians cherish their heritage and their old traditional dishes; they present them in their occasions. They protect their origins and roots, and uphold their identity and never leave their right. Palestinians's residents perform their role with dedication towards their families, homeland and society.

Questions about the story of Safed

The first scene
- What did Abu Ahmad draw on the dirt?

The second scene
- Count the names of some well-known trees in Safed as mentioned in the story.
- Who is Safed's founder? What's the name of the famous mountain on which it was established?
- What does Safed mean, why it was given this name?
- Mount Meron (Jarmaq) is located near the city of Safed, it is the highest mountain in Palestine, could you through the Internet search engines discover to which tribe does Mount Meron (Jarmaq) belong? Name four of the famous mountains of Palestine?

The third scene
- What are the main features of Safed's houses and roads?
- What were the characteristics that differentiate Safed's people than others?

The fourth scene
- Why did Safed people allow the Jews to live between them?

The fifth scene
- What is the name of the heroic leader who freed the city of Safed from the hands of the Crusaders in the famous Battle of Hittin?

The sixth scene
- Mention two of Safed's landmarks that were established in the Ottoman era.
- Over the years, Safed has witnessed a revival trade and exports. Mention some of the goods in which Safed was famous, as stated in the story.

The seventh scene
- Safed is famous for its delicious dishes and traditional sweets, mention three of them.
- Each city of Palestine has its own traditional costume, describe Safed's women's costume.

The eighth scene
- Mention the names of the mosques and the only church that still stand in Safed.
- Why do Zionists intentionally insult religious sanctities in Safed?

The ninth scene
- Why did the Zionists Haganah defeat the Palestinians despite their victories in the first rounds?
- External activity: stories of the Palestinian's Nakba and their displacement from their land are too many; do you know anyone suffered the pain of this displacement? How can you document and publish their story?

The tenth scene
- External activity using various search engines on Internet:
- Safed was the main station for the revolutions of the heroic Palestinian people. Mention the names of the four Palestinian revolutions against British colonialism and against the Zionist immigration to Palestine before its occupation.
- By reading the story of the student "Abu Ahmed's

granddaughter" and the journalist "Khuloud", what can a person offer to his homeland in hard times?

The eleventh scene
- What is the (Awda) Scout team's aim behind the establishment of camps for the people of the Palestinian cities?
- Why did Abu Ahmad feel so proud and happy?
- The (Awda) Scout team organized a series of events to enter joy into the hearts of the participants in the camp, mention some of them as stated in the story.
- Mention some of the traditional Palestinian games as listed in the story.

The thirteenth scene
- Describe the warm reception the scouts have organized for the camp's guests.

The fourteenth scene
- What was the surprise that awaited the guests in the big tent?
- Send us an e-mail expressing your feelings about the project that is going to be established by people of Safed towards Palestine? Do you find this a positive action towards the homeland?

Terms and definitions of the story of Haifa and Safed:

The olive tree:
A blessed old tree, spread in Palestine for thousands of years, its fruits (olive), and from it (olive oil) is extracted.

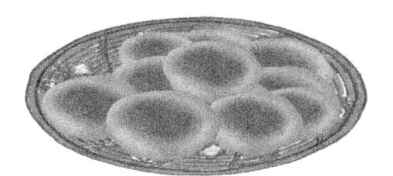

Almnakish:
It is a kind of pies on which oil and thyme are placed.

The key to return:
is one of the important symbols through which Palestinians express their commitment to return to their homeland and houses seized by the Zionists.

Windflowers:
(known as Hannoun or Dahnoun)
a flower spread in Palestine largely, it has glamorous colors, the Palestinians sing about it in their traditional and popular songs.

Sage: (*known as Maramia*)
Aromatic herb grows in Palestine, smells good, and has many health benefits, Palestinians love, and often drink with tea.

Saj:
Iron tin used in the preparation of tasty bread on the fire of coal, is part of the Palestinian heritage.

Wonder Box:
a closed box with circular holes, the viewer puts his eyes on those holes and sees images, driven by the storyteller, while telling an interesting story.

Hakawati:
a man moving between the neighborhoods; meets people to tell them interesting stories.

Al-Hakoura:
The name Palestinians use for their house's gardens, it includes some trees and important plants.

Melaya:

a piece of cloth the women of Safed wore over their elegant clothes, with their bright golden colors, interspersed with black lines.

Tabe' bread:

A local Palestinian bread, made using a special mold, which reflects amazing decorations and geometric shapes. The mothers used to make it on public occasions and holidays.

Ma'amoul molds:

Wooden molds with distinctive geometric shapes which the mothers used in order to prepare the most delicious kinds of Eid cookies.

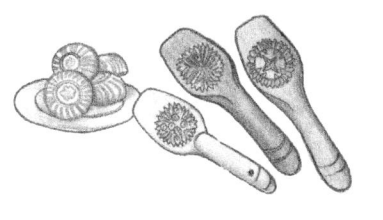

150